Cyrus the Great

The Enthralling Life of the Father of the Persian Empire

Free limited time bonus

Stop for a moment. We have a free bonus set up for you. The problem is this: we forget 90% of everything that we read after 7 days. Crazy fact, right? Here's the solution: we've created a printable, 1-page pdf summary for this book that you're reading now. All you have to do to get your free pdf summary is to go to the following website: **https://livetolearn.lpages.co/enthrallinghistory/**

Once you do, it will be intuitive. Enjoy, and thank you!

We forget 90% of everything that we've read in 7 days...

Get the free printable pdf summary of the book you've read AND much, much more... shhhh...

Enter Your Most Frequently Used Email to Get Started

DOWNLOAD FREE PDF SUMMARY

© Enthralling History

Table of Contents

Introduction

Writing was already common in the Middle East by the time of Cyrus the Great, creator of the Persian Empire in 550 BCE. And yet we have extraordinarily little factual and firsthand information about Cyrus the Great from contemporary Persian sources, except for the famous Cyrus Cylinder and a few inscriptions.

Most of the inscriptions are viewed as propaganda and are attributed to Darius the Great in the name of Cyrus, as he and later Persian rulers wanted to benefit from Cyrus's legacy. Scholars believe that Darius ordered the invention of the Old Persian cuneiform script in 521 BCE. He called it the Aryan script. These propaganda inscriptions are written in Old Persian, so they could not have been ordered by Cyrus. They are often inscribed in three languages—Old Persian, Elamite, and Akkadian—and simply state, "I am Cyrus, an Achaemenid king," to emphasize the Achaemenid family ties that Darius relied on to legitimize his rule.

The inscription of "I am Cyrus, an Achaemenid king" in Old Persian, Elamite, and Akkadian.

The most important and genuine Cyrus inscription is the Cyrus Cylinder. It was inscribed after the conquest of Babylon. It mentions the taking of Babylon, but its value lies in the proclamation of Cyrus's own values, intentions, vision, and actions. The cylinder talks about the liberation of the exiled peoples and slaves of the Babylonian Empire, which included the Jews. For this reason, Cyrus, or Koresh in the Jewish and Christian texts, is the only non-Jewish person to be called "Savior" in the sacred scrolls of the Jewish people.

A problem that crops up with the finer details of the Persian Empire's management is that Darius and his administration records and propaganda provide most of the information. The sum of it is that we use writings of ancient historians to extrapolate data for periods that are hazy or not described sufficiently in extant firsthand records. Those historians often did not really know much about the Persian Empire's methods of ruling. They often applied their contemporary observations and knowledge to previous times. That is especially the case for the Achaemenid Empire in regard to Cyrus II and Darius I.

It remains a monumental undertaking to sort fact from fiction, especially since Cyrus became a legend during his own lifetime. The embellishment of his life story started during his life and continued, with the first Greek historians recording tales of his ventures and achievements that had been passed down by his family, friends, and enemies. These later accounts are colored by the worldview of the cultured and learned Greek and later Roman historians and geographers. Admiration for Cyrus the Great from Persia's enemies, specifically the Greeks, must surely indicate he was a truly extraordinary figure who commanded respect and reverence as the father of the Persian Empire. He deserved to be called "Cyrus the Great."

In tracing the course of Cyrus's life, we are often left with choices between fact and fiction in the accounts passed on by ancient writers. Do we give the folk tales the benefit of the doubt because they could have happened? They were humanly possible and could have happened in real life. Cyrus was essentially a superhero but did not do superhuman things.

It often takes reading between the lines and an understanding of the historical context and contemporary environment of a historical figure to interpret their decisions and actions. For that reason, we have included various versions and viewpoints of the same events so you can see, feel, and understand the thrill of figuring out the people, culture, stories, and events of the past that have influenced humanity for generations.

At times, interwoven facts can be extracted from the tapestry of historical accounts and corroborated by annals and chronicles of contemporary rulers of nearby regions. Most of what we know of Cyrus the person comes from later accounts and extrapolations from records of contemporary nations. Some contemporary chronicles, like the Nabonidus Chronicle, roughly support the account of the conquest of Babylon, for example. This specific document, though, is fragmentary, with missing and unreadable pieces. The way in which both Cyrus and Nabonidus are portrayed indicates that it might have been written by priests of Marduk, the patron deity of Babylon, who hated Nabonidus and were glad to get rid of him. They also saw Cyrus as a liberator because he gave them their temple rights back, and they wanted to curry favor with him.

This book will serve partly as an overview of ancient life and times before, during, and after the life of Cyrus the Great. It is not limited to the accounts of the ancient historians about Cyrus the Great, as it includes brief histories of the worldviews, religions, and political and societal conditions of that time and the eras before and after it. Understanding these things will help you to understand how and why Cyrus the Great is still an icon today. His vision for a just, fair, and free society for all humanity echoes through the ages as an ideal that modern societies across the world should be striving to achieve.

Chapter 1:
The Persians before Cyrus

Setting the Scene: The Ancient Near East in a Time of Turmoil

It was a time of great upheaval across the ancient Near East. Widespread, drawn-out droughts caused hunger, and hunger made people desperate. Desperate people who have nothing to lose steal, protest, and riot. They look for a culprit—someone or something to blame. Anarchy spreads, and governments fall. Crime and unrest roll like waves across the sea of humanity, recognizing no borders and no authority as they move on and on to find water and food.

This situation waxed and waned across the ancient Near East and farther afield for several centuries from around 1200 BCE until around 900 BCE. The period is known as the Bronze Age Collapse. The fallout lasted for several centuries in some areas, such as Egypt, where the Third Intermediate Period officially started in 1070 BCE and only came to an end in the 7th century BCE.

Deep and clear rivers flowed out of the pure mountain snow from which they sprang, collecting more water from tributary rivers on their journeys to the seas, such as the Mediterranean, the Black Sea, the Caspian Sea, Lake Van, and other lakes. These waters, which allowed human populations to flourish, their flocks of livestock to increase, and farmers to cultivate and irrigate their crops, dried up. They did not flow into the great life-sustaining and navigable rivers like the Nile, the Tigris, and the Euphrates any longer. Those great rivers slowed and shrank to mere streams or dried up in places. Nomads became raiders of the movable possessions of yesterday's friends, neighboring tribes, and farther afield into settled lands and urbanized cultures. During this time of scarcity and unrest, they settled with their families and livestock wherever there was a chance of bettering their lives—a trickle of water could sustain them for at least a while.

Large urban centers of once-mighty nations depopulated because there was no food left in the cities, and farmers could not supply enough even for themselves. Soldiers deserted and joined the raiders. Rulers lost their power. Great dynasties were ousted and replaced, at times by outside nations and at times by internal strife. When things settled down again, borders were redrawn. Underdogs and new nations were in charge. Those vast empires that had conquered states, which were obliged to contribute copious amounts to their ruling empire's income in goods and raw materials, lost control. The empires did not have the power to crush revolts in their own territories, let alone try to bring outside nations back into the fold.

In Egypt, the country went through a bleak intermediary period. In Mesopotamia, Assyria and Babylonia managed to hold on to a semblance of power, albeit under new dynasties. Egypt and the rest of the Middle East were invaded by nomads, semi-nomads, and the Sea Peoples. The invaders were held off in some cases, but many re-invaded, conquered, and settled the land. At the end of the tumultuous period, the old kingdoms were gone, and new ones had taken their place.

Origin of the Persian People

Around the end of the 2nd millennium BCE, nomadic tribes from Central Asia and the steppes migrated to the Iranian plateau and spread into the valleys and hills of the country we know as Iran today. The reason for the several waves of the southward drift of nomadic groups is not entirely clear. It could have been the extreme and long-lasting droughts, population growth, or strife between tribes and chiefdoms, although it is likely all three factors played a role. There had been several similar small and large migrations of Indo-Europeans, Semites, and other groups with still unidentified origins and heritage, like the Sumerians, in previous centuries and even millennia.

The nomadic tribes of migrants in previous eras were mainly cattle and sheep herders, but now they included horse breeders from the steppes. They included Indo-European tribes that originated from the steppes in the north from around the Danube River and up to the Ural Mountains. Scholars are still trying to figure out the exact people groups and their origins via linguistic and DNA leads, but efforts are complicated by the mixing, diffusion, and other types of blending of the settled residents and the newcomers from before, during, and after this period. The newcomers were often already a blend of various ethnic groups, including Indo-European, Indo-Iranian, and diverse Semitic tribes from several different places, with people coming from as far as the Mediterranean lands and islands, Anatolia, Central Asia, and East Asia.

An important link in the archaeological record is the tribes with a penchant for horses—for breeding, milking, riding, fighting, and pulling agricultural equipment and wheeled transport. The peoples of the Eurasian Steppe, east of the Ural Mountains, are believed to have domesticated and trained horses for riding as early as 3500 BCE. The similarity in domesticated livestock and etymology—roots of words, phraseology, the types and names of agricultural tools, and names of people and places—have often provided scholars with a definitive clue in a people group's origin and movement. Today, researchers are greatly assisted by innovations and cooperation between various fields of science in the analysis of ancient DNA, bioarchaeology, paleogenetics, and other related fields.

Tribes that became the large kingdom of the Medes were part of the migrations of this era. They settled in the northeastern part of modern-day Iran, where their first king, possibly Deioces, built his capital, Ecbatana (today's Hamadan). At the peak of their power, the Medians had many vassal states in Anatolia, northern Iraq, and Syria, including the lands of the loosely knitted Persian tribes to the south.

Cyrus II of Persia (better known as Cyrus the Great) overthrew King Astyages, the last king of the Medes, between 550 and 549 BCE (these dates come from the Nabonidus Chronicle and ancient historians) with the help of high officials and commanders of the

Median court. The Medes did not lose their influence, though, as they remained by the Persians' side. The Persians and the Medes, in fact, became united in the empire. It is understandable if we remember that the Medes and Persians were of the same stock and language and cultural affiliations from the time before they entered Iran. One may also assume that the cooperation of high-level Median officials in Cyrus's victory over Astyages bound them together. It is obviously also the origin of the expression for an unbreakable law being referred to as "a law of the Medes and Persians."

The Persians

The tribes who would become the Persians moved farther south on the Iranian plateau than the Medes upon entering Iran. They began to take over some Elamite territory on the southern border of the Medes and other settled groups in the southwest of Iran and neighboring regions. It is generally accepted the Persians were Indo-Aryans from the Caucasus and the Caspian Sea areas. These tribes had spread as far eastward as South Asia (India). This latest wave of migrations moved into eastern Mesopotamia and the southwestern Iranian regions.

The Assyrian king, Shalmaneser III, mentions the Parsua around 825 BCE amongst tributary states in the southwest of today's Iran. It is generally assumed the people named Parsua on a black obelisk found in Nimrud and in other Assyrian and Babylonian cuneiform references refer to the Persian tribes. The Persian tribes were not united at this time. They were grouped into chiefdoms and later kingdoms. Shalmaneser III says that twenty-seven of their kings paid tribute to the Assyrians during his time.

After Cyrus succeeded his father Cambyses I as king of the city-state of Anshan, he set about uniting the Persian tribes, thus creating the Persian kingdom. According to Xenophon, another ancient Greek historian, there were twelve Persian tribes. He states the Persians raised their children from childhood to respect their elders and learn justice, discipline, and self-control above all other characteristics.

To the Persians, justice included fair and just laws against all the crimes that we view as crimes today, from stealing to assault and slander. But they also included ingratitude as well because they believed that trait to be shameless and at the root of many evil deeds. They were taught the traits of self-control, respect, and discipline by example, looking to their teachers, parents, officers, and elders as role models. Overindulgence and greed were unacceptable in their culture.

Cyrus was raised in Anshan by the Persians from the age of ten, according to Herodotus, and he was well versed in their culture and curriculum. As a teenager, he traveled with his mother to Ecbatana to visit Astyages, his grandfather. He charmed Astyages, his court, and the Median people to such an extent that he was begged to stay behind for a while when his mother returned home to Persia. This suited him because he was eager to learn horseback riding, which was not popular in Persia because of its hills. In addition, his grandfather, the king, promised that if he stayed, he could do and have anything he pleased.

Cyrus explained to his mother that he was better than anyone else when it came to Persian customs and that there was much to learn from the Medes. He stayed and learned the customs and skills of the Medes whilst bedecked in splendid robes and jewelry, as was their custom, which greatly differed from the more austere habits of the Persians.

Cyrus was a natural leader, and people wanted to please him and be close to him. It was thus easy for him to unite the Persians when he became king. Again, it is Xenophon who tells us that Cyrus grew up to be the most handsome and charming of all men.

The Beginning of the Achaemenid Dynasty

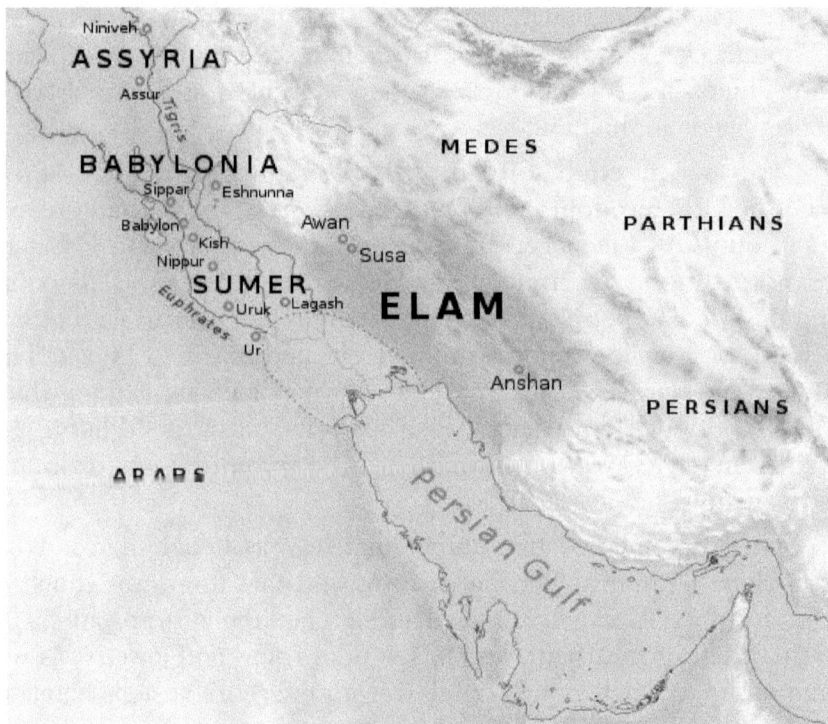

Anshan, the seat of the Achaemenid clan of the Pasargadae tribe, where Cyrus grew up

File: Near East topographic map-blank.svg: SémhurFile:Elam-map-PL.svg: Wkotwicaderivative work: Morningstar1814, CC BY-SA 3.0 <https://creativecommons.org/licenses/by-sa/3.0>, via Wikimedia Commons; https://commons.wikimedia.org/wiki/File:Elam_Map-en.svg

Anshan was one of the local cities taken over by one of several kindred Persian tribes when they settled in Iran. The Persians in Anshan were ruled by kings who traced their lineage to an ancestor named Achaemenes from the Pasargadae tribe. Scholars do not know whether this person was real or mythological, but the Persians derived the name of the Achaemenid Empire from his name.

It is generally accepted that Achaemenes was the father of Teispes, who was the father of Cyrus I, who was the father of Cambyses I, who was the father of Cyrus II or Cyrus the Great. Again, scholars have a problem with identifying and linking the names of the rulers in the various source materials. The name of the first Achaemenid king of the Pasargadae tribe was Phraortes I, according to Herodotus. According to the Behistun Inscription of Darius, who was the third king after Cyrus II, the first king of the

Achaemenid tribe was Achaemenes. According to the Cyrus Cylinder, one of the few contemporary inscriptions of Cyrus's time, the dynasty started with Teispes, who was the second king of the dynasty according to the Behistun Inscription.

Close-up of the Behistun Inscription.

Nevertheless, Cyrus II of the Achaemenid clan was the king of the Pasargadae tribe, and he eventually united the Persian tribes and built the Persian Empire. He first united the Persian tribes to throw off the Median yoke and then set out on a conquest across Anatolia, the Levant, and eastward through Central Asia and beyond. One by one, he conquered kingdoms and empires in all directions until his empire became the biggest the world had seen up to that time. Due to these widespread conquests north, south, east, and west, one of his titles in inscriptions was "King of the Four Corners of the World." His son and heir, Cambyses II, went on to conquer several more realms and carried forth that title, as did Darius I, another great Persian king.

The Achaemenid dynasty lasted until the Persians were conquered by Alexander the Great in 331 BCE.

Mythology and Religion

It is unclear what religion the ancient Persian tribes took with them to Iran, but it is presumed to be of a polytheistic nature, as that was common in the areas from and to which they migrated. In fact, polytheism was practiced around the world then and for millennia before that time, according to the plethora of myths that were eventually committed to writing. A mother goddess and several gods and goddesses for different natural and heavenly phenomena were prevalent across the Middle East and the rest of the ancient world.

Cyrus the Great depicted as a mythological being on a pillar in Pasargadae.
Nima Boroumand, CC BY-SA 4.0 <https://creativecommons.org/licenses/by-sa/4.0>, via Wikimedia Commons; https://commons.wikimedia.org/wiki/File:Cyrus_the_great.jpg

By the time of Cyrus's birth, a monotheistic religion, Zoroastrianism, was firmly rooted in the area, and Cyrus was ostensibly a follower of this religion. The dates mentioned for the beginning of Zoroastrianism are lost, although the religion began sometime between 1500 BCE and 700 BCE. The concepts of a struggle between good and evil, heaven and hell, angels and demons, a judgment day, and a final revelation, which can be found in the Abrahamic and many other faiths, stem from Zoroastrianism.

A man thought to have been part of the immigrating tribes into Iran had a vision while participating in an initiation ceremony. He was around thirty years old at the time, and his name was Zoroaster in Greek or Zarathustra in ancient Persian and Iranian. A supernatural being named Ahura Mazda appeared to Zoroaster during this vision.

Ahura Mazda, the supreme being of Zoroastrianism.
https://commons.wikimedia.org/wiki/File:Ahuramazda.jpg

He taught Zoroaster that he was the one and only god. He had created everything and was the only supreme being. Ahura Mazda explained to Zoroaster that the worship of many gods was wrong and that he alone, as Lord of Wisdom, was to be worshiped. Ahura Mazda is depicted as a male deity with wings or a winged vehicle.

Although Cyrus was devout in his religious pursuits, always making supplications and offerings before and after battles, he never tried to enforce his religion on conquered peoples. He incorporated and openly sacrificed to the local gods when in other countries. In fact, religious freedom is one of the basic characteristics for which he and his empire is remembered. Cyrus did not rely on priests to make sacrifices and supplications to his god, as was the common practice of rulers at the time; he was trained by his father and others to perform the ritualistic practices himself.

The legacy of Zoroastrianism, which was the religion of Cyrus's family, is still visible today in the fire temples, although after the long Muslim reign, there are very few practitioners left. Near the city of Yazd in Iran, there is a fire temple where a so-called eternal flame has been burning for centuries. Although it has been moved several times, it is believed to have been continuously burning since at least 470 CE.

The Persian Empire followed Cyrus's examples and doctrines and became known for its religious tolerance and freedom for all peoples to follow their own cultural practices. Cyrus practiced as he preached, ruling with truth and righteousness as his guiding light whilst respecting other people, their cultures, and their beliefs. He was, and still is in some places, called the father of the Persian people.

Key Figures

Astyages

The last king of the Medes was Astyages. His daughters were married in diplomatic unions to several other kings, linking royal houses in that part of the ancient Near East. One daughter, Mandane, was married to Cambyses, the king of Anshan. Astyages's brother-in-law was Croesus, the fabulously rich king of Lydia, who is remembered in the simile "as rich as Croesus."

The Medes had a tribe of wise men, the Magi, who interpreted dreams and signs. At the time, people were quite superstitious. Herodotus recounts a story verging on the edge of mythology about Mandane. When she was born, Astyages had a dream that the Magi interpreted as a warning that her offspring would rule the world, including Astyages's kingdom. A later dream was again interpreted as the same omen.

Astyages tried to prevent this by marrying Mandane off to Cambyses, the crown prince of an obscure far-away kingdom, and when she gave birth to a son, he arranged for the child to be killed. The child was saved and later became Cyrus the Great, who eventually ruled the known world. Luckily for Astyages, Cyrus was a magnanimous ruler who forgave his grandfather and looked after him until his death. Astyages was buried in the Persian capital of Pasargadae.

Cambyses I and Mandane

Cambyses was the son of the king of Anshan in Persia, a vassal state of the Medians. He was married to Mandane, daughter of Astyages. They became the parents of Cyrus the Great. According to Herodotus, Cambyses was known as a good man from a good family with quiet habits. This was why Astyages chose him as a husband for Mandane, as he assumed that his docile nature would rub off on his offspring and prevent a threat to Media.

Astyages obviously did not know about the strength of character that would be built in his grandson through the educational system of the austere Persians.

Harpagus

Harpagus was the Median nobleman who saved Cyrus's life when his grandfather Astyages wanted the baby killed. The cruel Astyages tricked Harpagus into eating the flesh of his only son at a feast after he discovered that Harpagus did not kill Cyrus as a baby when he had ordered him to do it.

The devasted Harpagus did not show his shock and grief but bided his time for revenge. When the time was right and Cyrus was grown up, he reminded Cyrus of his grandfather's plot to kill him and assured him that most of the Medians were ready to welcome him and join him in overthrowing Astyages.

Thus, if there was no Harpagus, or if Astyages had chosen a different courtier who was prepared to do his bidding to kill the newborn infant, there would be no Cyrus the Great!

Cassandane

Cyrus the Great's wife, Cassandane, was from the Achaemenid clan like him. She is said to have been the great love of his life. The Nabonidus Chronicle records that there was a six-day mourning period for everyone in the Persian Empire when she died in 538 BCE. She was buried in the royal garden at Pasargadae, close to the tomb of Cyrus.

One of her daughters, Atossa, was married to her son Cambyses (Cambyses II) and later to Darius the Great (Darius I). Atossa was the mother of Darius's son, Xerxes, who became king after Darius. Talk about keeping it in the family!

Cyrus Influencers

The most prominent figures of the Persian Empire that Cyrus created were his advisors. He surrounded himself with men from all social classes and nationalities whom he deemed fit and able in wisdom and decision-making. He even included his erstwhile enemies. These councilors were called together when serious decisions had to be made. Cyrus would lay the known facts before them, and those who had any suggestions for or against his suggested solution could then freely voice their thoughts and views on the matter. In this way, Cyrus was able to evaluate options from several different angles before deciding on the best course of action

Of these men, a few proved to be outstanding councilors. If we believe Herodotus's and Xenophon's accounts, then Croesus of the Lydians became one of these councilors after Cyrus conquered his country. Some other accounts state that Croesus was killed in battle or put to death shortly after Cyrus conquered his capital, Sardis. Yet, according to Herodotus, Cyrus kept Croesus close and often, if not always, asked for his opinion before making hefty decisions.

Harpagus, the Mede who was instrumental in saving Cyrus as a baby from his grandfather, was another of Cyrus's loyal and trusted advisors and generals. In fact, Harpagus brought many erstwhile Mede vassal states that strived for independence after Cyrus's conquest of the Medes back into the new fold. Harpagus went on to conquer more Anatolian, Bactrian, and other independent kingdoms for the growing Persian Empire, while Cyrus marched on the eastern and southern kingdoms with visions of totally conquering Elam, Babylon, and eventually Egypt.

Cyrus's habit of gratitude, appreciation, and humble requests for advice from his men ensured that he was respected and protected by the most loyal of men. His own Persian friends and advisors were always willing to protect him with their own lives. Advisors were selected from conquered peoples to help with local regions, and they soon learned to respect and like Cyrus as much as his own people because he treated them with respect and diplomacy.

Chapter 2: Cyrus's Early Life and Mythological References

Timeline of Cyrus the Great's Life

Estimated Dates	Occasion	Place
c. 600 BCE (other sources 590–580 BCE)	Birth of Cyrus II	Anshan, Persia or Ecbatana, Media
c. 590 BCE	Cyrus sent back to his parents at age ten	Anshan, Persia
c. 559 BCE	Cyrus takes over from his father Cambyses I (abdication) as king of Anshan	Anshan, Persis (Fars Province, Iran)
c. 550 BCE	Cyrus unites Persian tribes and creates Achaemenid Empire	Persis (Fars Province of Iran)

c. 550–549 BCE	Cyrus invades Media and captures Astyages	Ecbatana
c. 547 BCE	Cyrus conquers Lydia and takes their capital and king Croesus	Sardis, Anatolia
c. 540 or 538 BCE	Cyrus conquers the Elamites	Susa, the capital of the Elamites
c. 547–530 BCE	Cyrus creates satrapies and establishes a successful administration system for a large empire	Iran, Mesopotamia, ancient Near East, Asia, Anatolia
c. 539 BCE	Cyrus conquers Babylon	Babylonian Empire
c. 530 BCE	Cyrus campaigns against Massagetae tribes	Central Asia and Zagros Mountains
530 BCE / 529 BCE	Death of Cyrus II	Asia or Persia

Cyrus Becomes king of Anshan

Scholars are not in agreement with the role of Anshan in Cyrus's life. The controversies are mainly around the prominence of Anshan in Cyrus's titles. Ancient sources always name him as king of Anshan as opposed to king of Persia, such as on one of the best-known artifacts of Cyrus's reign, the Cyrus Cylinder. Firm historical facts are scarce, as there are few contemporary written records from primary Persian sources.

Several ancient writers after the time of Cyrus ventured into the mire of myths and legends surrounding his birth and as a young man, similar to myths and legends about many other great figures of the ancient past. It seems the ancients were compelled to create at least some kind of miraculous or wonderous stories around such figures, as no mere ordinary mortals could achieve the success and greatness with which they are credited.

Herodotus's Account of Cyrus before the Empire

Herodotus (484 BCE–425 BCE) recounted tales of Cyrus the Great's birth and childhood in *Histories*, with his usual caveat that he was only repeating what he had been told. To Xenophon (431 BCE–354 BCE), Cyrus was obviously a hero and idealized ruler. Xenophon even devoted eight volumes, the *Cyropaedia*, subtitled "The Education of Cyrus," to Cyrus the Great.

What all the accounts have in common are the details of his parents. Cyrus was the son of the crown prince of Anshan, Cambyses I, and a Median princess, Mandane. Anshan was an old Elamite city that had been usurped by one of the Persian tribes, the Pasargadae. At this time, the disunited Persian tribes were tributary states of the Medes.

Mandane was the daughter of the Median king, Astyages, and her mother was Aryenis. Aryenis was the daughter of the king of Lydia and a sister of legendary King Croesus. Astyages was the last king of the Median Empire.

The Medes were civilized and educated people, although they also seemed to have been rather cruel and strict. They had skilled astronomers, mathematicians, and scribes, but they were also superstitious. They had a tribe or class of sages, the Magi, who interpreted signs and dreams. When Mandane was born, her father Astyages had a dream that she urinated to the extent that it covered the whole world. The Magi were called to interpret the dream. They conferred and said that Mandane would have a son who would grow up to take over the world, Astyages's empire included.

Astyages believed them and set about creating a plan that would stop this from happening. When Mandane reached marriageable age, he married her off to the crown prince of Anshan, an obscure and far-away kingdom to the southwest. Then he had yet another dream. This time, an olive tree grew out of Mandane's womb and covered the entire world. The Magi agreed that it predicted the same foreboding message. When Astyages received the news that Mandane was pregnant, he summoned her to his court when her child was about to be born so that he could make sure it would not live to threaten him and his empire one day.

He took Mandane's son as soon as it was born and gave it to his trusted vizier, Harpagus, with orders to kill the baby. Astyages did not tell him that it was Mandane's child. The astonished Harpagus saw the baby was dressed in royal funeral clothes, bedecked with gold. He could hear the wailing in the palace when he was summoned and gathered that it was Mandane's newborn son. He had to obey his king, not just out of loyalty but also because he would face death if he disobeyed. Harpagus discussed the matter with his wife, and they both agreed he could not kill the little prince.

Harpagus went in search of one of the cowherds of the royal cattle and gave the baby to him. He ordered the cowherd, Mitradates, to take the baby into the mountains so the wild animals could kill it. It so happened that the cowherd's wife was pregnant. She had delivered a stillborn infant that very day. Mitradates and his wife conspired to switch the babies. They quickly switched the clothes of the two infants, and the cowherd took his own stillborn boy into the mountains instead. After three days, he sent word to Harpagus that the deed had been done.

Harpagus sent a messenger to view the dead infant, who confirmed the baby was indeed dead. Harpagus confirmed to Astyages that the boy had been killed as requested. Meanwhile, the cowherd and his wife raised the boy as their own. We do not know what the boy's name was, but Strabo, another ancient Greek historian, says he was called Agradatus by his adoptive parents. Cambyses I renamed him Cyrus after he was returned to his parents. Cyrus (or, at this time, Agradatus) grew up in a little rural village where his adoptive parents lived, believing that his parents were Mitradates and his wife.

According to Herodotus, when the boy was ten years old, he was happily playing with the other village children. They decided to play a game where they would elect a king, and this king would then tell each of them what to do. Because Cyrus was popular, he was chosen as their king. He turned out to be a clever and capable king, appointing each of his more capable playmates to a leadership role. They would be responsible for gathering their own teams to perform their tasks with them.

One of the boys, whose father was a high official in Astyages's court, refused to obey him. Cyrus and his friends gave him a thrashing. This boy went running to his father, who was as angry as he was. How dare the son of a cowherd order him around and then have the audacity to beat him up for not obeying! The father took his son to the king to show him the lashes on his son's shoulders. The king summoned the cowherd and his son. Cyrus took over his adoptive father's explanation and clearly told the king what had happened.

The king was perplexed that a mere cowherd's son could be so unafraid and forthright in explaining the matter to him, the king! But he seemed to recognize traces of himself in the boy. He ordered everyone, including Cyrus, to leave the room. He demanded that the cowherd stay behind, though. Astyages intimidated the cowherd, who broke down and told him the whole truth. Hiding his anger, Astyages then separately questioned Harpagus.

Seeing the cowherd inside the palace, Harpagus realized the story was out and resolved to come clean. Astyages acted as though he was actually relieved because the matter of his grandson's death and subsequent estrangement from his daughter had been a heavy burden on him. The Magi confirmed that he did not have to fear his grandson any longer when Astyages consulted them about the whole saga. Astyages acted as though he had forgiven his vizier for the deception, but in his mind, he planned an act of hideous revenge for the deceit. On the advice of his Magi, Astyages sent Cyrus off to his parents in Anshan.

Xenophon's *Cyropaedia* does not include the story of Cyrus's birth and life as the son of a cowherd. He places Cyrus in Persia from birth until his early teens when he visits Astyages with his mother and then stays behind to learn Median customs. His grandfather, Astyages, is upset when Cyrus eventually concocts a story that his father, Cambyses I, is ill and has to go home to Persia. According to Xenophon, this lie kindles Astyages's wrath to the extent that he instigates war against the Persians.

Stepping toward Greatness

Herodotus says Astyages sent Cyrus to his parents in Anshan after he was assured by the Magi that Cyrus, now a ten-year-old, was no longer a threat to him. Cyrus learned about the whole story of his birth, the betrayal of his mother, and Astyages's attempt to have his own grandchild murdered by the Medians sent by Astyages to escort him.

Cyrus was reunited with his overjoyed parents in Persia. He effortlessly fell into the culture and was a keen student of all that he could absorb from their education programs. Xenophon later described this in great detail in his *Cyropaedia*. Despite Xenophon's biased admiration of Cyrus and his veering off into a treatise to describe an ideal ruler's qualities rather than a realistic one, he gives us a solid idea of the values and systems of the Persians, specifically the Achaemenid culture into which Cyrus was now fully entrenched.

Etymology and Mythology

Much has been made of the origin of Cyrus the Great's name. Both ancient and modern writers have analyzed, considered, and debated how and why Cyrus was named Cyrus II. However, this may be an exercise in futility. Firstly, Cyrus was named after his grandfather, King Cyrus I, so the name did not originate with him. All the insightful and graceful meanings that are read into the name when attaching the name specifically to Cyrus II could not have been thought out by his parents, as Cyrus developed these attributes later.

Secondly, we do not know what Cyrus's name was for the first ten years of his life spent as the son of a cowherd (if that was how he indeed spent his early childhood). The name Cyrus was probably already planned by his real parents for a future crown prince, just as Cyrus named his firstborn son Cambyses (II) after his father. When Cyrus was returned to his parents from the dead, so to speak, they automatically called him by the name given to him at birth.

As for the name of the Achaemenid clan to which he belonged, there are no records of the founder of this clan. This man was called Achaemenes on various inscriptions. He could have been a mythical figure or a prominent member of the Pasargadae tribe who was chosen as the chief or leader over the kings of all the tribes at a time when the clans were loosely knitted together. This could have applied during times of upheaval, especially during the migrations to Iran with the other Persian tribes.

The nomadic herders across the ancient world, to which the tribes of the later Persians belonged, left few permanent or extant artifacts and structures behind as far as is known. They seldom had permanent seasonal settlements in the vast open grazing lands or mountains and valleys to the north. And yet, with modern technology, many previously unknown structures have been discovered over the past fifty years or so. There may be many more unexpected Göbekli Tepes to come.

Chapter 3: Taking over the Median Empire

The Medes

Among the migrants to the lands of today's Iran after c. 1000 BCE were the Medes, who settled in the northwest of Iran. Although the tribes settled there around the turn of the millennium, the Medes only came to unite and expand their territory into a kingdom and later an empire beginning around the 8th century BCE. Most of what is known about the Median Kingdom is based on Neo-Assyrian and Babylonian records.

Since the beginning of the Median Empire (675–549 BCE), its kings seem to have followed a harsh pattern of despotic rule. Its first king, Deioces, tricked the Median tribes into believing they needed a judge, and the position soon became that of a king. Since Deioces had long ago proved himself to be a good judge, he knew they would naturally select him. Although he first came to attention as a wise judge within his own tribe and later the rest of the Medes, he became a power-hungry and arrogant tyrant.

Deioces had the people build him a magnificent palace on a hilltop in a new city known by the Greeks as Ecbatana, today's Hamadan in Iran. One of the ancient writers wrote that it was known as the most magnificent palace and city of its time. The city was surrounded by seven concentric walls, each painted in a different color. Deioces lived in splendid isolation and allowed only certain people near him, partly as a means of intimidation. In his mind, he was too important to be seen by just anybody. He expected those seeking his judgment to wait outside and hand their messages to his aides, who would then bring them to Deioces and return his replies to the petitioners.

The Medes were pestered by the Scythians to the north and paid tribute to the Neo-Assyrians, who helped to protect their territory against invaders. When the Neo-Assyrian Empire was in decline, the Medians were one of its tributaries that stopped paying tribute. In 612, the Medes, in alliance with a few other subject states, conquered Nineveh and brought about the end of the Neo-Assyrian Empire.

The language of the Medes, like that of the Persians, belonged to the western branch of the Indo-Iranian branch of the Indo-European language group. The Medes consisted of six tribes spread over an area of northwest Iran and neighboring territories. Their capital city was Ecbatana (modern Hamadan). Scholars do not agree if Media remained only a kingdom or whether it held the status of an empire.

Astyages, the last king of the Medes, was only the third Median king, as the line of kings had been broken by a period of Scythian rule. Herodotus's account of Astyages's cruel punishments includes the birth story of Cyrus and the cruel revenge on Harpagus, his vizier, to whom he slyly served his own son as a meal as punishment. These two, Harpagus and Cyrus, would unite when the time was right to exact their revenge on Astyages.

Harpagus and Cyrus: Double Revenge

Astyages was the master of his own demise through his harsh and, at times, exceedingly cruel treatment of his subjects and courtiers. Harpagus had never forgotten that he had unknowingly been served the fried and boiled flesh of his only son. And then, after he had indulged in the meal, the king presented him with the feet, hands, and head of his son. Harpagus bided his time and waited for his revenge, and in this case, revenge worked out for him, lest we forget the warning of Confucius that one should first dig two graves before setting out for revenge: one for oneself and one for the object of your revenge.

When Cyrus was grown up, Harpagus contacted him. He reminded Cyrus that his grandfather had set out to have him killed when he was born and that he, Harpagus, was instrumental in saving him. He suggested that Cyrus might want to take revenge, hinting that if Cyrus set out on this venture, the Medes would welcome and join him in overthrowing Astyages. Harpagus had already set about quietly convincing his Median colleagues that it was time to rid themselves of Astyages. They were ready to join Cyrus if he decided to attack.

Whether myth or fact, neither Xenophon nor any other ancient source confirms Herodotus's story of the conspiracy between Cyrus and the Medes to overthrow Astyages. Harpagus somehow managed to send Cyrus this very confidential message. The message was clearly treason, and Astyages was not a forgiving king. Herodotus's story says that Harpagus selected his most trusted servant for the task. He caught a hare, cut a slit in its stomach, and inserted the message. Then he sewed the slit up again. The servant was given the hare inside some nets so he could act like a hunter with his catch. The plan worked, and the servant got safely past the guards and delivered the message to Cyrus.

Growth of the Persian Empire

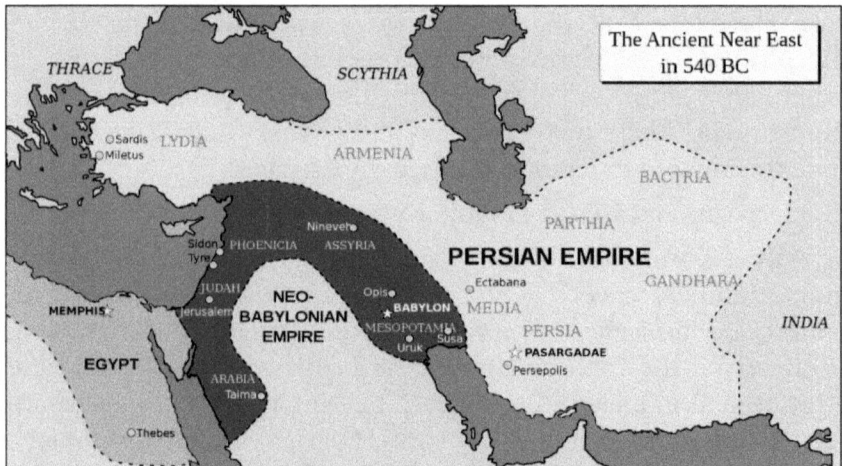

The ancient Near East in 540 BCE.
https://commons.wikimedia.org/w/index.php?curid=5061033

According to some sources, Xenophon included, Cyrus was still the crown prince of Anshan in Persis or Persia. Cambyses I, his father, was still the king and thus had the final say over any Persian troops. But Herodotus states he was king of the Pasargadae tribe by this point.

In any event, Cyrus received the message from Harpagus. He then had to decide how best to get the Persian tribes to unite and revolt. According to both Herodotus and Xenophon, Cyrus was extremely popular, but he was not in the habit of ordering his friends and others around, despite his position. He followed a more subtle approach, telling the Persians that Astyages, as overlord of the Persians, had made him leader of the troops. He then asked the tribal leaders to come to him the next day with their sickles. Cyrus set them to clear a difficult piece of land, and they toiled at it all day. He then sent them home and asked them to return the following day.

On the second day, Cyrus treated them to a lavish banquet. Afterward, he asked them which day they preferred. They naturally chose the second day. Cyrus promised them that if they followed him in revolting against the Medes, they would be treated like this often and be showered with many more blessings. If they did not want to follow him, they could be assured that challenging work lay in store for them. The Persians did not only promise to join Cyrus because of his tantalizing promises but also because they had been resenting paying tribute to the Medes for a long time.

The newly united Persians under Cyrus marched on the Medes. Astyages tried to summon Cyrus to meet with him when he heard about the advancing army. Cyrus replied that he would be seeing him sooner than he thought. Astyages was consumed with concern, and without giving his past dastardly conduct against Harpagus a thought, he appointed Harpagus commander of his forces.

When the armies met, all of those with whom Harpagus had colluded deserted the Median army to join the Persians. Most of the others fled. The small Median group that took up the fight was quickly overcome. Cyrus and his forces attacked Ecbatana, where Astyages was. He was captured and put in chains. Harpagus taunted him bitterly over his son's vile death and the cruel trick that had him eating his own son's flesh.

Uniting Conquerors and Conquered

Cyrus was already displaying his admirable and gracious style of dealing with his conquests. He took Astyages home with him and kept him there until he died. Cyrus was now king of the Medes and the Persians. According to some ancient sources, though, Astyages was killed after the battle in his capital city, Ecbatana, today's Hamadan in Iran.

This is where the different accounts really get confusing. According to some, Cambyses I was still alive and king of Persia. And in Ecbatana, the capital of Media, Cyaxares II, son of Astyages, now became king of the Medes, which became a vassal state of Persia. There was no bad blood between Cyrus and Cyaxares, who also happened to be Cyrus's uncle. In addition, Cyrus then supposedly married a daughter of Astyages, which would mean that he married his mother's sister. Surely, she would have been a bit too old for the able and vibrant Cyrus, who would go on to father several children.

This particular account has Cyrus going on campaigns against the Neo-Assyrian Empire and the Babylonian Empire on behalf of his uncle Cyaxares II.

Again, we must look to Herodotus, despite his embroidered version of many events, as it is generally accepted and corroborated by contemporary chronicles that the Babylonians and their allies had already conquered the Neo-Assyrians and took over their territories and vassal states before Cyrus was born.

Cyrus set out on his own after conquering Lydians to take on Elam and Babylon, with thoughts of taking over Egypt at a later stage. Egypt was eventually conquered by the Persians under Cyrus's son and heir, Cambyses II.

Pasargadae: The New Persian Capital City

After Cyrus conquered the Medes, he selected the plain where the two armies met for battle as the site for a new capital city of the Persian-Median Empire. The extensive plain on which it was built lies approximately ninety kilometers (fifty-six miles) northeast of the modern city of Shiraz. It was declared a World Heritage Site by UNESCO in 2004.

The name of the city was probably chosen by Cyrus in honor of the Persian Pasargadae tribe, to which his Achaemenid clan belonged. There are also opinions that its name was derived from the meaning of the word "Pasargadae," which could have been "throne of Pars" or "strong club."

The citadel was a large platform-like construction on a low hill that provided an unobstructed view across the plain to see any approach on the city. This may have been a crucial lookout point because the city was not enclosed by defensive walls. Below the citadel, there was apparently a magnificent garden.

Pasargadae was built in a unique style, which would become specific to the Achaemenid Empire. The large public buildings were positioned across the city as opposed to grouping them together in the city center. The large open site of Pasargadae now contains ruins of a *caravanserai* (an inn for travelers and their animals in the arid regions of Asia and North Africa) dating to the 14th century CE. The ruins of the ancient city include several garden features, decorated pillars, ruins of at least three palaces for different purposes, pavilions, water channels, and a high stone tower, the latter of which is considered to be the tomb of Cambyses II, the son and successor of Cyrus who only ruled for eight years.

Cyrus's tomb stands out in its simplicity. It resembles a small ziggurat with a chamber on top. According to ancient texts, Cyrus designed the tomb and selected its site between his private palace and the park-like garden. The garden was described by a companion of Alexander the Great, Aristobulus, as having all kinds of trees, running water features, and lawns. Aristobulus also said that, at that time, there was a Persian inscription on the tomb identifying it as the tomb of Cyrus:

"O man, I am Cyrus son of Cambyses, who founded the empire of Persia and ruled over Asia. Do not grudge me my monument." Aristobulus's writings are no longer extant, but the words are quoted by several later ancient writers, such as Arrian and Strabo, who credit Aristobulus as the source.

Cyrus the Great: Father and Husband

Cyrus was called the father of his people in several ancient sources. In his personal life, of which we know little, he was a father and a husband. At some point in his life, Cyrus married

Cassandane, a fellow Achaemenid, so we can assume that it happened after his extended visit to his grandfather, Astyages, in Ecbatana. Cassandane is still celebrated today in Iran. She is said to have been the great love of Cyrus's life. Cassandane is thought to have died in 538 BCE.

Again, according to some later sources, Cassandane was just one of Cyrus's wives, but in other accounts, she was his only wife and the mother of his children, Crown Prince Cambyses II, Smerdis (Bardiya), Atossa, Artystone, and, according to some sources, Roxane. It is said that Cyrus mourned her passing for the rest of his life. The Achaemenid Empire, according to ancient contemporary records, officially mourned her passing for six days in 538 BCE. Cassandane was buried at Cyrus's new capital city, Pasargadae; some sources say she was buried next to the place planned for Cyrus's tomb.

Xenophon complicates matters of Cyrus's wife or wives and sons even further. He has Cyrus giving a long speech on his deathbed. In the end, he asks his sons to say goodbye to their mother for him. The sons here are called Cambyses and Tanyoxarces, and they are his chief heirs, with Cambyses inheriting the empire and Tanyoxarces several satrapies (provinces). Thus, his wife—or his first wife, the mother of Cyrus's eldest son Cambyses—was still alive.

If we use Xenophon's account of Cyrus's death, Cyrus could not have mourned her as some other ancient historians claimed because he sent her greetings from his deathbed! Here again, we come across one of the problems with different names between various sources, as Herodotus and others call the second son Bardiya or Smerdis, and here he is called Tanyoxarces. It must be mentioned that the name differences were often because of translations from Old Persian to the writer's language.

And then there is the question of Amytis as a wife of Cyrus. It appears from some sources that after overthrowing the king of the Medes, Cyrus may have married his mother's sister, and thus another daughter of Astyages, to legitimize his claim to the throne of the Median Empire. This does sound a little unnecessary because he already had the support of the Median elite and, by all accounts, was popular amongst the people. His armies had routed the small Median force that did not join the generals who fought with the

Persians. Cyrus already had a close tie with the Median ruling family because Astyages was his grandfather. Astyages did not have a son to inherit the throne. So, why did Cyrus have to marry his aunt?

This Amytis could have been much younger than her sister, Cyrus's mother, Mandane. She is mentioned by Ctesias as demanding retribution for the death of Tanyoxarces (Tanaoxarces), who is called Bardiya and Smerdis by other authors, after his brother, Cambyses II, murdered him. When this did not happen, she killed herself by drinking poison.

The Children of Cyrus the Great

If you thought the royal houses in the Middle Ages were atrociously inbred, have a glance at some of the ancient ruling families.

Cyrus's eldest son, Cambyses, succeeded him. Atossa, the daughter of Cyrus and Cassandane, married her brother, Cambyses. Another daughter, Roxane, also married Cambyses II. She apparently died in Nubia during Cambyses II's Egyptian campaign. Atossa married their other brother, Smerdis, afterward. But this Smerdis was, in reality, a Mede usurper posing as Smerdis, the son of Cyrus. The real Smerdis had been murdered by Cambyses II out of jealousy before he embarked on his Egyptian campaign. After Darius I, who came from another branch of the Achaemenid family, and his co-conspirators reclaimed the throne for the Achaemenid dynasty, Darius married Atossa. Darius also married Atossa's full sister, Artystone, and their cousin, Parmys!

Darius and Atossa had four sons, of which one—Xerxes—would succeed him. Artystone and Darius had three children. She was said to have been Darius's favorite wife. He even had a golden statue of her in their garden.

Xenophon left us Cyrus's beautifully worded final speech that was addressed to his sons when he was on his deathbed. If only they had followed his advice, history might have turned out differently. But then, when did children ever follow the wise council of a parent?

"Consider again that there is nothing in the world more nearly akin to death than is sleep; and the soul of man at just such times is revealed in its most divine aspect and at such times, too, it looks forward into the future; for then, it seems, it is most untrammeled by the bonds of the flesh.

"Now if this is true, as I think it is, and if the soul does leave the body, then do what I request of you and show reverence for my soul. But if it is not so, and if the soul remains in the body and dies with it, then at least fear the gods, eternal, all-seeing, omnipotent, who keep this ordered universe together, unimpaired, ageless, unerring, indescribable in its beauty and its grandeur; and never allow yourselves to do or purpose anything wicked or unholy."

Chapter 4: The Conquest of the Lydian Empire

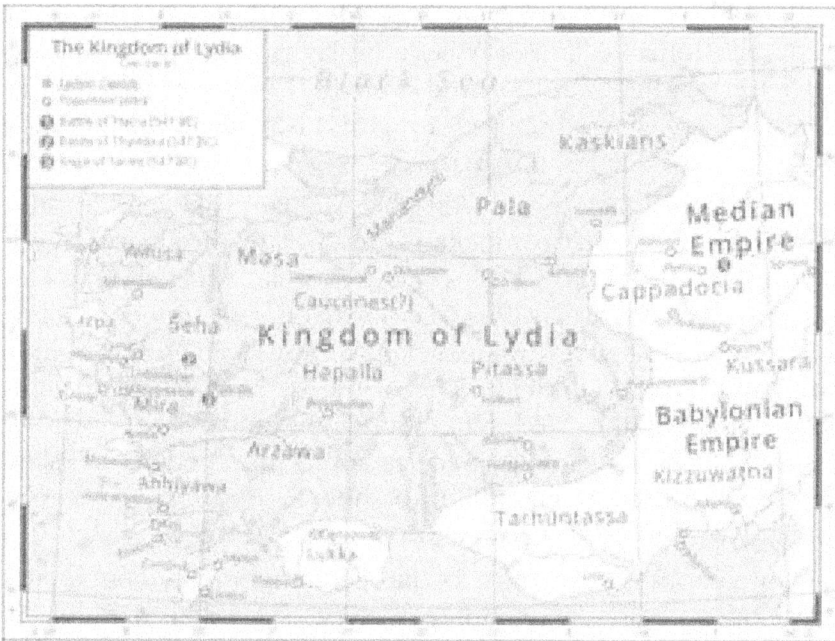

Lydian Kingdom under King Croesus, which was conquered by Cyrus in 547 BCE.

Cattette, CC BY 4.0 <https://creativecommons.org/licenses/by/4.0>, via Wikimedia Commons; https://commons.wikimedia.org/wiki/File:Map_of_the_Kingdom_of_Lydia.png

After the Medes

Whichever ancient historian we believe, at least they seem to agree that Cyrus's next war was fought against Lydia. Lydia was the kingdom of the famous Croesus, to whom the idiomatic expression "as rich as Croesus" refers, at least in the English language. Lydia was situated in Asia Minor, thus to the north of the Levant or ancient Near East in modern Turkey. Croesus had a large army of mostly mercenaries. Many of the surrounding nations paid tribute to Lydia since they were afraid of angering King Croesus.

The Lydians had made several incursions into Media and vice versa over the years before this war. When Croesus's father, Alyattes, was still king of Lydia, Media and Lydia were engaged in bloody battles and skirmishes for five continuous years. This war stopped in its sixth year because of the paranormal fears of both nations when a solar eclipse happened one early afternoon during heavy fighting. It was recorded this particular eclipse had been predicted by one of the Seven Wise Men of Greece, Thales, from the Greek Ionian island of Milesia (today's Miletus). To seal their peace treaty, which was brokered objectively by two outside sources, Croesus's father was obliged to give his daughter, Aryenis, to Astyages of the Medes in marriage.

After Cyrus had thrown off the Median yoke and captured Astyages, Croesus felt compelled to avenge his brother-in-law. He had two other objectives up his sleeve as well. This rich king's land was crossed by a river with a seemingly endless supply of alluvial gold, but like many of the super-rich, Croesus wanted more—in this case, land! So, he attacked some of the states that had previously been vassals of the Medes but were now under Cyrus. Croesus destroyed the settlements and captured the people as slaves. Croesus also thought it prudent to show his strength and stop the young Cyrus before he became too powerful.

Now, Croesus, like most of his contemporaries, consulted an oracle or two before he committed to war. He did his due diligence and found the Oracle of Delphi, also known as Pythia, at the Temple of Apollo, was the most respected. So, Croesus gathered together a massive gift of treasures and sent his representatives to Delphi to ask the oracle if he should go to war against Cyrus and if he should gather allies to join him.

Pythia replied in her usual obscure manner that could be interpreted in several ways by an unwary listener, especially after the fact. The answer was that Croesus would destroy a great empire if he went to war against Cyrus. The second question was answered in a separate reply, and she advised Croesus to ally himself with the strongest Greek states.

Croesus assumed Pythia predicted he would destroy Cyrus and the forces of Media and Persia, but he had to get a strong Greek ally. Croesus made a pact of mutual defense with the Spartans and prepared for war with Cyrus. Lydia's vassal state in Phrygia made overtures to Cyrus and became a Persian vassal state instead. Croesus used this as an excuse to go to war with Cyrus.

His forces encamped at an ideal spot in Cappadocia and proceeded to attack this newly acquired vassal state of the Persians. They destroyed everything in their path, from the fields to the settlements, and took the people as slaves. Their booty included the nearby city of Pteria, which was the capital city of the province.

Meanwhile, Cyrus, who had heard of Croesus's escapades, gathered his forces and prepared to meet Croesus. On his way, his armies gathered more and more soldiers, as many were eager to join this new charismatic leader. They met in a province of Cappadocia, and a battle commenced in which many soldiers from both sides perished. The battle was still undecided by evening when the troops retired to their respective encampments.

Croesus's Miscalculations

The next day, Cyrus's troops did not turn up on the battlefield. Croesus assumed the Medes and Persians had gone home since the fighting season was over. He was convinced that he did not win the battle outright only because his army was outnumbered by Cyrus's men.

At this time in history, the Lydian soldiers had everything going for them. They were known to be brave, strong, and battle-hardened. Moreover, they were well equipped, and their greatest strength lay in their cavalry. They were skilled riders and fought from their horses with long, deadly spears that they wielded with great precision. The only obvious reason they did not gain an outright victory must have been as Croesus determined: the Persians' superiority in numbers. However, if one takes into account Xenophon's remarks about the hero worship and desire to please Cyrus that all his men felt toward him, you might wonder if there was perhaps a psychological difference in the driving force behind the armies on this battlefield. Most of Croesus's soldiers were mercenaries driven by payment for their services.

As Croesus set out to return to Sardis, the magnificent Lydian capital, he resolved to call in reinforcements from all his previous allies to remedy the matter of sheer numbers before the battle season resumed in spring.

From his palace on the fortified hilltop in Sardis, he sent the mercenary troops home and dispatched messengers to his allies to join him or send reinforcements in spring. He also sent messengers to Sparta, Babylonia, and Egypt, with whom he had previously concluded defense treaties, to come to his aid when the war resumed. He speculated this would be in around five months when spring started.

Cyrus, meanwhile, had discussed matters with his officers and advisors, and they decided the time was ideal for attacking the unsuspecting Croesus.

Croesus was very surprised and unprepared when Cyrus turned up on the plains outside his capital. He gathered his forces and marched out to meet him. Once the forces were set up in battle formations facing each other, Cyrus could not help but be concerned over his enemy's magnificent cavalry display. One of his commanders, the Mede Harpagus, suggested they should use the camels of the baggage trains and mount them with soldiers as the first line of attack. Horses, he said, were sorely spooked by camels. It would sow confusion amongst Croesus's cavalry when the horses reared and threw their riders off to flee the battlefield.

Cyrus followed this excellent advice and sent the camels to the front. When the two armies met, the pride and strength of Croesus's army—the cavalry—were thrown into disarray. But Croesus's men still fought valiantly until they had to retreat into their city.

Sardis Besieged

Cyrus laid siege to the city. Each side watched and waited, one from the open plain, the other from the city walls. Who would give up first? Winter was coming, so the Lydians in the city were adequately provisioned for many months. Croesus and the Lydians assumed it would be a long siege, but they knew they could hold out as long as they needed to. On the other hand, the army on the unprotected plain had only their tents to protect them against the chilly winter winds of the treeless plain. They had only the food they carried with them.

THE SIEGE OF SARDIS.

Siege of Sardis, engraving by Jacob Abbott, 1803–1879.
https://commons.wikimedia.org/wiki/File:The_Siege_of_Sardis.jpg

The Lydians were laughing and taunting the Medes and Persians down below. They felt safe and cozy in their well-fortified city. The messengers that Croesus had sent to his allies before the siege would by now have arrived at their destinations. Reinforcements would be arriving in five months, just as Croesus had requested of them. The mercenaries whom he had sent to their homes would also be back in five months when spring started.

Croesus felt safe and comfortable in his palace, where he could indulge in every luxury. Life could go on as usual. He was, after all, the richest man in the world and could wallow in lavishness since his city was safe and secure. According to legend, the city walls had been blessed never to be breached because the previous king, Meles, had carried a sacred lion around the walls. The legend was that this lion was born from one of his concubines. Meles carried the miracle lion cub around every nook and cranny, every inch of the surrounding wall, for this sacred protection—except where the wall was an extension on top of a sheer cliff face. But nobody could climb up there anyway.

Below the walls, out of reach of missiles and arrows from the city guards, Cyrus and his men were scanning the walls with sharp-eyed attention to find any vulnerabilities. The officers and men were considering any feasible way to enter, but no Lydian ever entered or left the city. Cyrus promised great rewards to the man who would be the first to climb the walls because that seemed the only way in.

One day, after two weeks of watching and waiting, one of Cyrus's men noticed a man from the city climb down the wall and the sheer cliff face to retrieve a helmet. He climbed skillfully back up the cliff and the wall. Furtively, the Persian crept closer when the man was gone. He tried to copy the Lydian's actions and managed to climb the same route. Other soldiers followed him, and soon, they were inside Sardis! The city was taken. By Cyrus's order, Croesus, who was hiding inside his palace, was not to be hurt in any way. He was brought unharmed to King Cyrus.

Cyrus built a large funeral pyre, and he set Croesus and fourteen young Lydians on top of this. As their captors were kindling the wood, Croesus, who had not spoken at all since he was captured, suddenly sighed and cried out the name of Solon three times. Solon (630 BCE–560 BCE) was one of the Seven Wise Men of Greece. Croesus had remembered the words of Solon that no living man was blessed. He obviously thought of his own multitude of blessings that he had taken for granted while always considering himself to be a blessed man.

Upon hearing all this, Cyrus was contrite, thinking of how he was in the process of putting another to death while thinking himself blessed, just as Croesus had. He realized that people could not count on any kind of security in life; one's circumstances could change in an instant. Cyrus ordered the fire to be put out. But by this time, the flames had taken hold, and try as they might, they could not extinguish it.

From the pyre, Croesus saw what was about to happen. Thinking of all the offerings, gifts, and riches he had bestowed on the Temple of Apollo at Delphi every time he consulted the oracle there, he called on Apollo. As if in answer to his plea, a sudden rainstorm quenched the flames, and the Lydian youths and Croesus were saved.

Treatment of Croesus after Defeat

Croesus standing in front of King Cyrus.
https://commons.wikimedia.org/wiki/File:Croesus_and_Cyrus.jpg

Afterward, Cyrus wanted to know why Croesus had, without being provoked in any way, attacked and destroyed Persian lands. Croesus fully admitted he was the only one to blame, for no man should desire war over peace. He added that sons buried their fathers during peacetime, but in war, fathers buried their sons. Croesus's reply and his actions on the stake made Cyrus aware that he was saved just in time from committing a cruel deed. According to both Herodotus and Xenophon, Cyrus resolved to keep Croesus by his side for his valuable counsel. And so, Croesus became a part of the advisory group that Cyrus always kept near when he wanted to hear other points of view while considering options and actions.

The usual controversies arise when other sources are consulted on the demise or, rather, subjugation of the Lydians by Cyrus. Bacchylides, a Greek lyrical poet, says that Croesus did not want to be enslaved by Cyrus after his victory of Sardis. He, therefore, built his and his family's funeral pyre and had a slave set it alight. Zeus put the fire out with a thunderstorm. Apollo then saved Croesus from the flames by carrying him off to the land of the Hyperboreans—a mythical kingdom beyond the northern edge of the known world. Hyperborea is thought to be a land of perpetual spring, a place that is beautiful and plentiful. It was generally interpreted as the land of the afterlife.

Cyrus Grows the Persian Empire Once More

Cyrus the Great, painting by Jean Fouquet, c. 1470.

After the defeat of Lydia, several of Lydia's vassal states stopped paying the required tribute. They were unaware that Croesus and Cyrus had reached an agreement that the Persians would not ransack Sardis if the Lydians freely shared their riches. Croesus also bequeathed all his income from the Lydian tributary kingdoms to Cyrus and the Persians. However, the kingdoms over which Croesus was overlord thought it expedient to take the chance of becoming independent. Cyrus soon crushed these revolts.

One of these other kingdoms, that of the Ionians, had been invited by Cyrus before his incursion into Lydia to join forces with him. They refused because they fully expected that Croesus would be the victor. The Ionians now quickly requested that Cyrus take over their overlordship under the same terms as they had before with Lydia. The Ionians lived in the cities and islands in the southeast of modern Turkey, in and around the Ionian Sea, most of which are today well-known archaeological and tourist sites, such as Ephesus and Priene.

Cyrus shrewdly messaged back the story of a flutist who expected the fishes, which he saw swimming in the clear waters, to join him on the beach to listen to the beautiful music he was making. The fish did not do so. The flutist then caught them in a net. Watching them jumping and flapping about in the net, he told them to stop dancing. It was too late now, as when he played for them before, they did not come to him. The Ionians understood his message.

The Ionians expected war. They fortified their cities and called the Ionian League to their sacred meeting place, a temple dedicated to Poseidon. They decided to send a delegation to Sparta to ask for assistance. The Spartans refused to join them. However, the Spartans sent a warning to Cyrus that he must stay away from the Greek territories, or they would punish him. Cyrus replied that he was not afraid of men who had a sanctuary in which to hold their meetings in a secret conclave. He implied that in that kind of council, deceit and lies reigned supreme. He added the Spartans would be better off forgetting about the Ionians and looking after their own people.

Cyrus left Sardis under the charge of one of his Persians. A Lydian was put in charge of Croesus's treasures, which he was supposed to deliver to Pasargadae's treasury. Cyrus was on his way back to Persia to plan further campaigns, with Elam and Babylon heading his list. A messenger arrived to inform him the Lydians, under the leadership of the Lydian left in charge of the treasury, had revolted against the Persian governor.

With Croesus's treasure in hand, the rebels under the Lydian had fled Sardis and were hiring mercenaries to help them drive the Persians out of Lydia. It seems the rebel leader had dreams of becoming king of Lydia. Cyrus sent one of his Median generals to quell the revolt. Croesus successfully talked him out of enslaving the Lydians as punishment. He advised Cyrus to forbid the Lydians from making or carrying weapons. He said Cyrus should order them to change their lifestyle so they could pursue peace and harmony instead of war.

Once this Median general subdued the Lydian rebellion, he set about conquering the rest of Anatolia and then pursued the Ionians. When he died of an illness during these campaigns, he was replaced by Harpagus, the same Mede who had helped Cyrus conquer the Median Empire. Harpagus was successful in conquering the nations to the north and east of Iran.

Chapter 5: The Fall of Babylon

Neo-Assyrians: Enough Is Enough

Before the time of Cyrus, the Medes and Babylonians had, at times, stood together against the mighty Neo-Assyrian Empire. The Neo-Assyrian Empire was a harsh overlord. After bloody and brutal battles, the Assyrians took conquered peoples, or at least huge numbers of them, as prisoners and resettled them elsewhere in exile. A good example of this would be the ten tribes of Israel in the 8th century BCE. They were deported by Tiglath Pileser III in 722 BCE from northern Israel and replaced with exiles from other countries.

The replacements were mostly Mesopotamian peoples. In this way, the Assyrians kept revolts of conquered peoples in their vast empire under control and to a minimum. They removed the rulers, the elite, and craftsmen from other conquered countries, leaving mostly just peasants behind. These exiled peoples were then spread amongst other conquered folks to be assimilated and lose their national identity.

There are magnificent reliefs of sieges and various deportations that were recovered from the Neo-Assyrian period at the palace of Nineveh; they are now displayed in the British Museum. At the settlement sites of these forced immigrants in Israel, clay tablets, pottery, and other cultural objects confirm that fairly large Babylonian groups were among the resettled and exchanged populations.

The Chaldeans in the Arabian Gulf, meanwhile, had grown strong. Around 626 BCE, their king, Nabopolassar, rid them of their Assyrian overlords. He crowned himself king of Babylon and set about restoring the erstwhile glory of Babylon. He revamped the infrastructure of the capital city, Babylon, and added new public buildings, temples, and irrigation channels, there and elsewhere in Babylonia, while keeping the Assyrians at bay. By the time of Cyrus and the Achaemenid Empire, the city of Babylon was one of the largest and most prosperous cities in the known world. The Babylonians and their allies had taken advantage of civil strife and attacked the Neo-Assyrians in 612 BCE. Nineveh, the Assyrian capital at that time, was taken in 609 BCE. The Neo-Assyrian Empire would never rise again.

At Last, Going for the Prize: Babylon

Nabopolassar had trained and educated his son, Nebuchadnezzar II, well in state affairs and warfare to successfully inherit and expand the Neo-Babylonian Empire after his death. Nebuchadnezzar became the most successful ruler of the Chaldean dynasty of Babylonia, but he was followed by weaker rulers. Cyrus finally marched against the last king of the independent Chaldean dynasty in Babylon when a rather weak and very unpopular ruler, Nabonidus, was on the throne.

According to Xenophon, Cyrus was sidetracked several times in this endeavor and only reached his destination after many other adventures. Herodotus, in his usual style of describing the ins and outs of every significant person and geographical aspect along the way, eventually describes the incredibly strong fortifications of Babylon. A third extant source for Cyrus's conquest of Babylon is the very fragmented and damaged Chronicle of Nabonidus. Out of these several sources, which, in truth, are extremely difficult to compare due to the usage of different personal and country names, historians have managed to put together a reasonable scenario of Cyrus's conquest of Babylon.

Sieges and Battles

The first major clash between the Persians and the Babylonians happened at the Battle of Opis, located northeast of Babylon. Nabonidus had sent a certain commander, Belshazzar, to intercept the Persians, but his forces were decisively beaten by the Persians.

According to some ancient sources, Belshazzar was the son and regent of Babylon when Nabonidus lived in Arabia for ten years. He was also the king or acting king whom Daniel of the Christian Bible had told that he had been weighed and found wanting and would be struck down that very night. Daniel, a Jew in exile, had been called by Belshazzar to explain text that suddenly appeared on the wall of his palace while he was having a party.

It seems Nabonidus was a bit of a coward, as he did not participate in the Battle of Opis. The remnants of his army fled back to Babylon. Nabonidus was hiding in Sippar and left the city to be attacked, fully expecting it not to be conquered and that he could return and remain king.

At last, the greater forces of the Persian armies arrived at Babylon and encamped a distance away from the city when Babylonian troops did not come out to meet them in battle. It must be kept in mind that several of Cyrus's armies, under the command of his trusted and loyal friends, were constantly busy in other regions of the Persian Empire, ensuring peace, nipping revolts in the bud, and conquering new territories.

At Babylon, Cyrus first planned to parade his troops right under the city walls. He was dissuaded by one of his companions and advisors, who suggested they march by at a fair distance. Cyrus wanted to gain knowledge and insight into Babylon's defenses and fortifications. He compromised by selecting a distance that was just far enough to be safe from enemy arrows and missiles from the city walls.

It was evident from Cyrus's own inspection that the tales of Babylon's unbreachable walls were true. Apart from the water-filled ditches that surrounded the outer walls of the city, the walls were thick and strong. Herodotus says they were built with baked clay bricks set together in tar and that the walls were up to fifty royal cubits deep (a royal cubit is about twenty-one inches or fifty-three centimeters). The soil dug from the trenches was used to make the bricks, and the tar came from another Babylonian city. Babylon was split in half by the Euphrates River, which was a ready supply of water. The city was also stocked with a good food supply in case of a siege.

On either side of the riverbanks were parallel walls with bronze gates that could be opened to give access to the streets. According to Herodotus, the city was filled with houses built three and four stories high. On one side of the city was the center, which was occupied by the royal palace, and on the other side was a sacred precinct with a temple for Marduk named the Esagila and a ziggurat. The ziggurat was topped with another temple for Marduk, the chief god of the Babylonians. This was known as Etemenanki (Home of the Foundation of Heaven and Earth), although Herodotus, being thoroughly Greek, called it the temple of Zeus.

Semiramis and Nitocris

An interesting tidbit about Babylon's defenses comes from Herodotus. Two queens in different eras are mentioned as contributing to the building and construction works of Babylon. Semiramis, whom ancient Greek writers mistakenly place as a ruler in Babylon (r. 811 BCE–806 BCE) instead of Ashur in Assyria, made drainage channels and canals across the wide open plain on which the city of Babylon was built. This stopped the Euphrates from regularly flooding the city and the plain.

The history of this woman is clouded in mystery. Ctesias describes her as half-goddess and half-human. According to myths, she was raised by doves. Other ancient writers attribute the famous Hanging Gardens of Babylon—one of the Seven Wonders of the Ancient World—to her. It is likely she was a Babylonian princess who married an Assyrian king, Shamshi-Adad V. After his death, she became regent over the Assyrian Empire until her son, Adad Nirari III, could take the throne. Her name was Sammu-ramat or Shammuramat, but the later Greek historians called her Semiramis. Most of what is written about her are legends, but she is clearly mentioned in Assyrian records and had her own obelisk in Ashur, Iraq.

The second queen mentioned by Herodotus is Nitocris (c. 550 BCE). Nitocris greatly strengthened the defenses of Babylon in numerous ways. She is said to have rerouted the mighty Euphrates River before it neared Babylon so that it flowed with several twists and turns, winding back and forth upon its previously straight course. This influenced the progress of any army approaching the city. Then she built reinforcements along the riverbanks to make them higher and sturdier. She also dug a basin deep enough to find the groundwater level so that water could seep into the basin and form marshland on the quickest route toward the country of the Medes, who, according to Herodotus, was her most dangerous enemy at the time.

In the city of Babylon, Nitocris bricked out the bed and banks of the Euphrates where it ran through the city. The boats previously used to cross from one side of the city to the other, but she built a bridge that was only open during the daytime. According to Herodotus, Nitocris had her tomb built on top of the main city gate with a luring inscription for some future ruler who really needed funds, saying they could open the tomb and take her burial goods. Somehow, nobody ever tried until Darius the Great came along. He found the tomb empty except for a note that said, "Wert thou not insatiate of wealth and basely desirous of gain, thou hadst not opened the coffins of the dead."

Cyrus took the city in October 539 BCE, using the river to breach Babylon's defenses. One portion of his troops was left in readiness at the site where the river entered the city, while he took the rest miles away to divert the river. The Babylonians were taken completely by surprise because all the activities of digging large trenches to divert the mighty and swiftly flowing Euphrates happened out of sight. And the water was diverted during the night.

It was the night of a national feast day in Babylon. By the time the feasting citizens noticed, the Persians were already amongst them. They had entered through the shallow riverbed and found many of the inside city gates in the river wall had been carelessly left open.

Cyrus Welcomed

According to the fragmented Nabonidus Chronicle, Nabonidus was absent from Babylon for extended periods. For example, he once lived in Tayma, a large oasis in the Arabian Desert, for ten years, ostensibly to subject Arabia. It may have been that he was too afraid to handle the ever-present palace intrigue and was as uncomfortable in Babylon as the people there were with him. Eventually, he returned to Babylon and was captured in his palace. According to the Nabonidus Chronicle, there was much bloodshed, especially among private citizens throughout the city. This fact can be questioned, as Cyrus had instructed the troops to order the people back into their homes, with a warning that only those caught on the streets after the fact or who resisted would be killed.

Cyrus was a man who craved peace rather than war, as attested by inscriptions on clay tablets that were excavated from several sites across his empire. One example comes from an inscription on a baked clay brick found in Ur by the British archaeologist Sir Leonard Woolley. It is now on display at the British Museum. It is inscribed in Babylonian and has Cyrus's various names and titles, along with a statement that he established peace in the land. It is dated to the 6th century BCE and was probably one of many that were used throughout the empire.

In this scenario, it follows that most of the people of Babylon welcomed Cyrus into their city. In addition, there were lots of foreign exiles present in the city and the country because the Babylonians had, since the time of their greatest king, Nebuchadnezzar, displaced the conquered peoples, similar to what the Assyrians did. But the Assyrians had often switched their captives with those of other conquered countries, while the Babylonians had them in their own cities amongst their own people. Naturally, these groups were jubilant to be rid of the Babylonian yoke and celebrated the conquerors.

With the conquest of Babylon, as happened after the conquest of the Medes and then the Lydians, Cyrus automatically became the overlord of its vassal states. In the case of the large Babylonian Empire, this included countries bordering the Mediterranean Sea, like Syria and Palestine.

Elam at Last

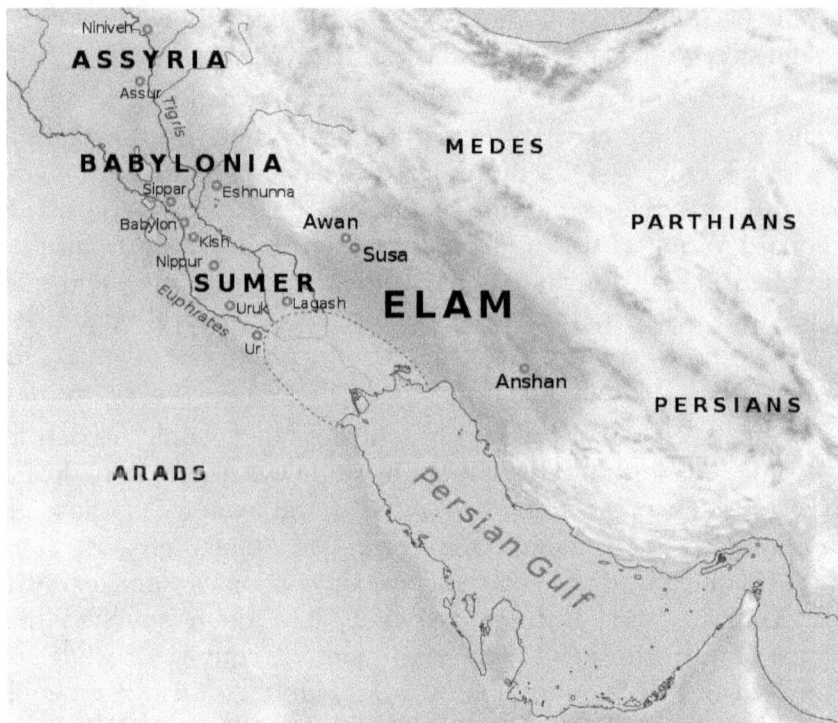

A map of Elam.

Although Cyrus had his sights set on Elam as one of his next targets when he left Sardis, he only conquered their capital city, Susa, sometime between 540 and 538 BCE, just before or just after the conquest of Babylon. The Elamites had fluctuated between greatness, being conquered by stronger nations, being vassals to several overlords, and being independent for more than a millennium. They were frequent raiders of neighboring nations and vice versa since the time of the Sumerians and the Akkadians.

At times, the Elamites were allied with other foreign powers in attacks on their neighbors. In around 1000 BCE, their capital city was conquered by the Babylonians. Their fortunes waxed and waned as vassals of Babylon. They developed their own script, which remains largely undeciphered, despite several claims of breakthroughs. Part of the problem is the minimal number of extant texts or inscriptions available to scholars.

In 645 BCE, Elam was conquered by Ashurbanipal of Assyria. He completely destroyed the city of Susa. It was subsequently rebuilt and repopulated over a relatively short period of just one century.

And then it was the Persians' turn. After Cyrus the Great finally conquered all of the Elamites by 538 BCE, Susa remained an important city in the Achaemenid Empire, acting as an administrative center. In fact, it became one of the three administrative capitals of the Persian Empire during the reign of Cambyses II (the son of Cyrus) and later Darius I. The other two administrative capitals were Babylon and Ecbatana.

Chapter 6: Ruling the Empire

History of Empires: Tyrants Fall

Cyrus realized that throughout the history of the ancient world, empires fell because it was impossible for one person to control vast territories of conquered peoples. So, he employed various methods to counter the mistakes of past emperors. Xenophon's *Cyropaedia* is especially helpful due to his account of Cyrus's background and education and analysis of Cyrus's successful rule that laid the foundation of the Achaemenid Empire.

The education system of the Achaemenid tribe, and by implication the rest of the Persian tribes, reminds one of modern-day Montessori and Ad Astra approaches. Xenophon describes the male education system, but many accounts from this time indicate that women had the same education and rights as men.

Xenophon says the public square in Anshan was divided into four spaces: one for boys, one for youths, one for mature men, and one for elders. Although Cyrus spent his first ten years in Media as the son of a cowherd (at least according to Herodotus), his innate intelligence and abilities allowed him to learn from each experience. After Cyrus was recognized and returned to his own family, King Cambyses and his wife, Mandane of Media, he was educated in the Persian ways.

The main lessons of the boys' section in the Persian town square centered around justice and discipline. Self-discipline and self-control were valued above most other traits. Presiding over each of the spaces in the square were twelve officers—one from each of the twelve Persian tribes. They were selected for their skills and abilities. These officers provided judgment and punishment when the boys laid charges against each other. Apart from charges of theft, robbery, assault, cheating, and other offenses that our laws generally include today, the Persians saw crimes stemming from ingratitude as the most serious. In their view, ingratitude caused selfishness, and selfishness caused most offenses and neglect of duty.

Cyrus The Great's Central Philosophy

"Whenever you can, act as a liberator. Freedom, dignity, and wealth – these three together constitute the greatest happiness of humanity. If you bequeath all three to your people, their love for you will never die " – Cyrus the Great, according to Xenophon.

The above quote shows the philosophy Cyrus had about life in general, and this included the way in which he ruled.

This philosophy would become central to how Cyrus ruled his vast empire of 2.1 million square miles (5.5 million square kilometers). It informed the doctrine that made his rule over such an empire manageable and prosperous in terms of innovations, business, and societal frameworks.

How Did Cyrus Conquer and Manage This Vast Empire?

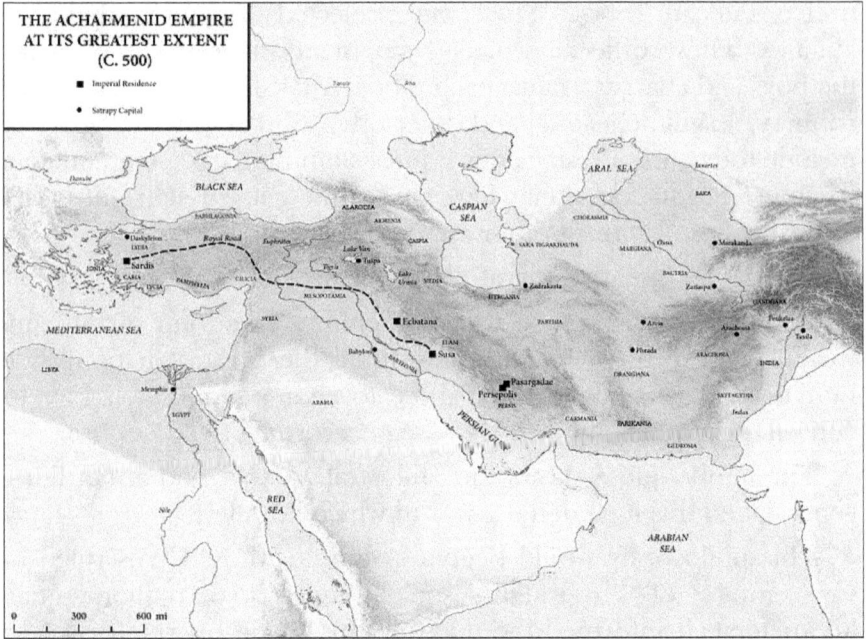

THE ACHAEMENID EMPIRE
AT ITS GREATEST EXTENT
(C. 500)
■ Imperial Residence
◆ Satrapy Capital

Achaemenid Empire.

Original creator: MossmapsCorrections according to Oxford Atlas of World History 2002, The Times Atlas of World History (1989), Philip's Atlas of World History (1999) by पाटलिपुत्र, CC BY-SA 4.0 <https://creativecommons.org/licenses/by-sa/4.0>, via Wikimedia Commons; https://commons.wikimedia.org/wiki/File:Achaemenid_Empire_at_its_greatest_extent_according_to_Oxford_Atlas_of_World_History_2002.jpg

The empire that Cyrus created spanned from the Mediterranean Sea in the west to the Indus River in the east. The Persian Empire was, without a doubt, the largest empire up to that time. Following the death of Cyrus, his successors, Cambyses II and Darius the Great, continued to expand the empire until it reached the Balkans, southeastern Europe, and Egypt. Cyrus the Great left the administration framework of the territories he conquered in place, although he made some adjustments and left people there that reported to him and his administration centers. He set up an unequaled structure to administer and manage this vast empire, and since the infrastructure and logistics were already in place, his successors simply had to maintain and improve the existing methods of rule.

The First Victory

Other versions of Cyrus the Great differ in detail from what we have looked at so far, which has mostly been from Herodotus and Xenophon.

After the death of his father, Cambyses I, Cyrus became king of Anshan. However, since Anshan was a vassal state of Media, he was not an independent ruler. Cyrus's kingdom paid tribute to the king of Media, who happened to be his maternal grandfather, Astyages.

In the Nabonidus Chronicle, a clay tablet exhibited at the British Museum in London, a scribe details the attack on Cyrus by his grandfather Astyages. The cuneiform text specifically states that Astyages launched an attack on the "king of Anshan." There are various accounts of this battle and who initiated it.

In the Nabonidus Chronicle, Ecbatana's mutiny and Astyages's capture are confirmed. Historians Herodotus and Ctesias wrote that Cyrus married the daughter of Astyages, Amytis, to pacify the Median vassals, including Saka, Bactria, Parthia, and Hyrcania. Herodotus also notes that Cyrus integrated Sogdia into his Persian Empire during his military campaigns against the rebels who wanted their freedom after Media was conquered.

Further Unification: A Family Business

Since Cyrus became king of all the vassal states that were previously under Media's rule, Parsa, which was ruled by his uncle Arsames, peacefully became part of the new empire. Cyrus left the governing of this city-state in the hands of his uncle. Hystaspes, Cyrus's cousin and son of Arsames, was given charge of Parthia and Phrygia. Cyrus united the Achaemenid kingdoms, including Parsa and Anshan, and made the budding Persian Empire a well-run family business.

Expansion

The occupation and takeover of Media was only the beginning of what would become Cyrus's vast empire. According to some accounts, Cyrus did not want to take over any neighboring kingdoms at this point. He was satisfied with running the Persian Empire, which now included Media. He was managing state affairs and governing successfully, so there was no need to go to war after squashing rebellions that broke out in Media's vassal states.

As was customary, Croesus, King of Lydia, sent regular messengers to the Oracle of Delphi to request advice from Pythia before momentous decisions. As is noted by Pausanias, a Greek geographer and scholar (110–180 CE), the magnificent gifts from King Croesus to Apollo and the Oracle of Delphi were a regular testament to his wealth and trust in her prophecies.

During one of these deputations to the oracle, Croesus was told he would "destroy a great empire" if he attacked the Persians. Croesus took this to mean that he would destroy Cyrus's empire. Croesus decided to attack Pteria in 547 BCE. Although Pteria was previously a vassal state of Lydia, it had declared its loyalty to the Persian Empire and Cyrus the Great.

When King Cyrus heard of the siege of Pteria, he gathered his armies and moved to defend the city. However, on his arrival, he found that Pteria had already been conquered and the citizens enslaved by Croesus. Croesus had burned down the city so that Cyrus could not use it as a strategic location from which to fight.

Croesus retreated to Sardis, assuming Cyrus would not follow. Cyrus did the opposite and attacked Croesus and the Lydian army at Thymbra. Cyrus conquered Sardis and brought an end to the Lydian Empire and the Mermnad dynasty. Cyrus spared Croesus's life, and Croesus became a part of the team of military advisors that Cyrus relied on.

The approximate end of the Lydian Empire is generally accepted as being 547 or 546 BCE. After the fall of Lydia, its vassal states in Anatolia, Lycia, Ionia, Cilicia, and Phoenicia became part of the Persian Empire.

Blueprint for the Persian Empire

Cyrus became the ruler of Anshan, then conquered the Median Empire with the Median general Harpagus by his side. This was followed by his conquests of the Lydian Empire, the Elamites and their capital of Susa, the Babylonian Empire, and further military expansions into Central Asia. These broad facts seem to be historically confirmed across most sources, both primary and secondary.

During Cyrus's thirty-year reign, he showed the qualities of being a great statesman and military leader, especially when it came to invading foreign territories. He would first approach the leader of the region with an option to negotiate the takeover in a non-violent manner. Only once his offer was declined would he declare war. Even in the event of war, Cyrus acted with humanity, as can be seen with King Croesus, who joined Cyrus's empire as part of a military advisory unit. Cyrus had the option of killing Croesus, as was customary at the time, but he did not.

A different version of the Babylonian conquest is that the ruler of Babylon, Nabonidus, fled to Sippar after Cyrus conquered Elam. Nabonidus left Ugbaru in charge of the army. Ugbaru, previously the governor of Gutium, changed allegiance. According to the Babylonian Chronicle, "Ugbaru, governor of the district of Gutium, and the army of Cyrus entered Babylon without a battle." Ugbaru is called Gobryas by the Greek historian Xenophon. He was appointed as the Babylonian governor by Cyrus after the Babylonian conquest.

Nabonidus was captured, but his life was spared, and he was sent into exile to live his life out in the region of Carmania. It is assumed that his co-ruler and son, Belshazzar, was killed during the taking of Babylon. Nabonidus was still living in exile during Darius the Great's rule.

Accounts of Cyrus and his military expansion campaigns were recorded as bringing "into subjection every nation without exception."

According to some historians, the Persian Empire always tried to negotiate with its enemies before engaging in battle, as battles were (and still are) costly in every respect, and Cyrus would rather attempt to get the enemy to surrender.

Sharing Power: How to Rule a Large Empire

Cyrus the Great was an ingenious statesman, charismatic leader, and military genius. This was because he was wise enough to surround himself with advisors who were specialists in their fields and knew the people and geographical areas they intended to enter.

After establishing his new capital, Pasargadae, in Fars Province of today's Iran, Cyrus refined the way of ruling and managing his vast Persian Empire. He showed great administrative prowess in the development of a socially acceptable and organized government.

By establishing a regional government system that reported to the central government, Cyrus managed to effectively administrate the Persian Empire. He divided it into twenty-six provinces called satrapies.

Satrapies

The Achaemenid Empire spread across most of West Asia and much of Central Asia, including areas of the Mediterranean and Hellespont (the Strait of Dardanelles in modern-day Turkey) in the west and stretching to the Indus River in the east.

Cyrus developed a system where each region became an autonomous province with a satrap or governor who represented him in each province. This system of provincial governments originated in the Median era around 648 BCE, and became more formalized and effective under the rule of Cyrus the Great beginning in 547 BCE.

Throughout the centuries, lands were ruled by the kings or emperors who conquered those regions—until Cyrus the Great, that is. Cyrus adapted previous styles of ruling to suit his own requirements. He likely studied how previous empires failed and avoided known problems.

Cyrus divided his empire into twenty-six provinces under satraps who ruled in his name. Each satrap had to be a guardian of the well-being of his people and territory. A satrap was responsible for law and order, tax collection, civil administration, and the selection and training of an army for each province that the king could call upon when the need arose. Additionally, Cyrus understood the need to honor the social and cultural activities of each nation. Oversight was left in the capable hands of the satrap.

Although the satraps had autonomous and broad powers over their provinces, there were many checks and balances in place to ensure the satraps did not overstep the line.

Delving Deeper

Cyrus the Great earned his reputation not only because of his military conquests but also due to his natural communication skills and his understanding of the human psyche. The basic method of ruling via a governor or satrap might not initially have been his idea. However, the extent of local autonomy, understanding of the local people, accountability of the satraps, and the systems of checks and balances in the administration of these satraps were due to his ingenious methods.

Five-Layer System

By the time of Darius, a five-layer system of governance was used. It is assumed that it was started by Cyrus and later refined and adapted to a more centralized system by Darius I. Cyrus knew there had to be checks and balances at all levels, as he had to ensure he could rule successfully and with maximum efficiency. The different hierarchies would run independently yet be interwoven to form a system of checks and balances on the satraps.

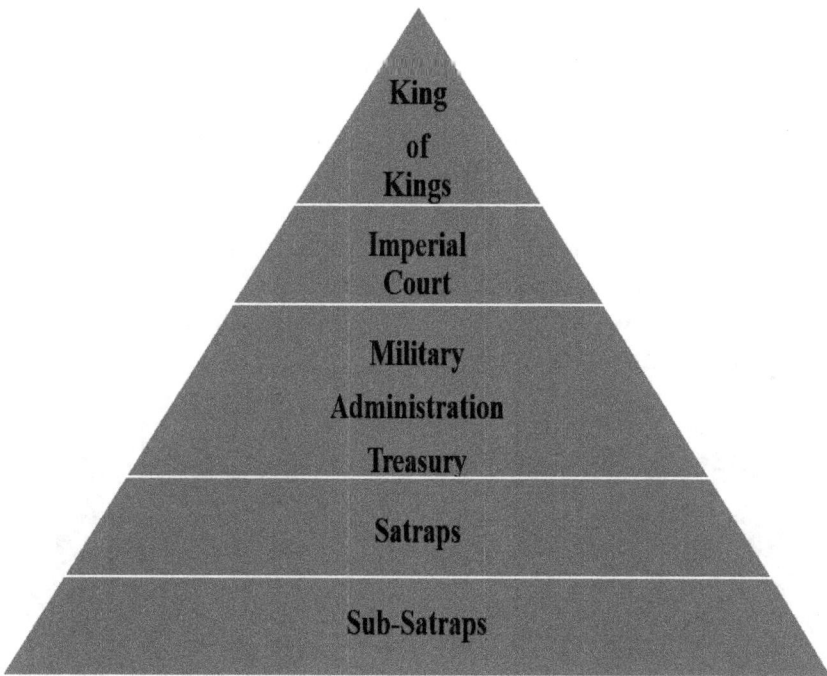

King
of
Kings

Imperial
Court

Military
Administration
Treasury

Satraps

Sub-Satraps

Five-layer system of rule of the Achaemenid Empire.

King of Kings

The monarch, in this instance, King Cyrus, was the supreme authority. He was seen to have no equal on earth, and his word was law. Theoretically, from this position of great power, the king could do as he pleased. However, for all practical purposes, he was supposed to be accountable to the imperial court.

Imperial Court

The imperial court was chosen from the nobility and elite citizens of the Persian Empire. These ministers played a key role in advising and counseling the king and kept a watchful eye on the satrapies. When selecting the members of his imperial court, King Cyrus again displayed his innovative ideas. He surrounded himself with the most loyal advisors selected from the Persians and from each conquered territory.

Military, Administration, and Treasury

The third tier of the hierarchy had immense responsibility and great power. They were the flexible yet permanent and immovable institutions that ran the day-to-day governance of the empire.

The famous army unit of the Achaemenid army, known as the Ten Thousand Immortals, was established by Cyrus the Great and formed the core security of the Persian Empire. Herodotus describes the Immortals as "heavy infantry," and the size was kept at a constant number of ten thousand soldiers. Beneath their robes, they wore scale armor. They used swords, large daggers, short spears, bows, and arrows, and for defense, they used wicker shields. These legendary Immortals are still a fascinating subject for Hollywood filmmakers today.

The Immortals, a photo of the 1971 celebration of the Achaemenid Empire in Iran.
https://commons.wikimedia.org/w/index.php?curid=7497892

The imperial administration's main objective eventually became profit and control. But, of course, over time, corruption and nepotism set in, obscuring Cyrus's high ideals of equality for all. Even Darius I, arguably one of the greatest rulers in history, appointed family members as satraps. Darius was also responsible for monetizing tributes and making it a compulsory fixed sum contribution, whereas Cyrus relied on willingly contributed "gifts" of goods and objects of value, often surplus production of what a country produced or precious metals and stones. Cyrus took a chance and trusted the loyalty of his subjects and their willingness to come to his aid whenever he needed them. In return, they looked up to him and called him their father.

Later, the reallocation of ownership of conquered lands from low-class citizens to the elite ensured the empire remained profitable for a while. This reallocation and upliftment of the elite class would eventually contribute to the fall of the mighty Persian Empire. The luxurious lifestyles of the elite began to cripple the economy. At that time, Cyrus was a distant memory.

Satraps

The satraps were the governors in charge of the empire's provinces and its administration, finance, law and order, and social and cultural activities. The satrap wielded the same amount of power over their regions as the king had over the empire. This essentially meant the satraps were extremely powerful in their own right. At times, a specific satrap that had governed his region well would be given a neighboring province to rule over, naturally increasing his income and power.

To maintain law and order, the satrap acted as the supreme judge in civil and criminal cases and was responsible for exacting justice. According to Xenophon, a satrap was also responsible for the safety and security of the interprovincial roads and had the right to put down rebels and bands that tried to rob travelers and postal workers on the Royal Road.

Here again, Cyrus was wise and allowed governors of conquered regions to continue their rule but insisted they adhere to the five-layer system of governance. Since they were already rulers of their local regions, they knew the culture, administration, and financial requirements to run their provinces successfully.

Sub-Satraps

The final layer of the Persian government formed a part of the satraps' "royal" court and was chosen from the local citizens, who knew the customs and traditions of their people. Their role was to advise and assist the satraps in integrating new taxation or administrative practices into the provinces. They would also advise on various subjects, such as religious practices, dress codes, and local traditions.

Modus Operandi

Some historians suggest that Cyrus's method of ruling a multi-national empire that tolerated ethnoreligious and cultural diversities emerged from necessity. He understood that enforcing a singular identity across such a diverse and large geographical area would result in constant conflicts.

As a form of monarchial rule, the methods used by King Cyrus were complex, flexible, and strategic while exemplary in terms of humanity.

Later kings abused the central bureaucratic form of governance. All positions under the king had to obey the monarch's command implicitly, whereas Cyrus negotiated outcomes. His commands were more like requests. One can only imagine that the legendary Ten Thousand Immortals would have been enough to keep the peace and enforce the law if called upon. Satrapies obeyed the monarch in every aspect of local governance and knew the result of rebellion or theft: the Immortals!

During Cyrus the Great's rule, no rebellions were recorded, and the respect he earned can be seen in the way he was reportedly viewed as a father by his subjects. There can be no greater honor than to see your ruler as a father figure.

George W. F. Hegel, a German philosopher, in his book *Lectures on the Philosophy of History,* describes the Persian Empire as "the first to pass away" and the people as the "first historical people."

"The Persian Empire is an empire in the modern sense—like that which existed in Germany, and the great imperial realm under the sway of Napoleon; for we find it consisting of a number of states, which are indeed dependent, but which have retained their own individuality, their manners, and laws. The general enactments, binding upon all, did not infringe upon their political and social idiosyncrasies, but even protected and maintained them; so that each of the nations that constitute the whole, had its own form of constitution. As light illuminates everything—imparting to each object a peculiar vitality—so the Persian Empire extends over a multitude of nations and leaves to each one its particular character. Some have even kings of their own; each one its distinct language, arms, way of life, and customs. All this diversity coexists harmoniously under the impartial dominion of Light ... a combination of peoples—leaving each of them free. Thereby, a stop is put to that barbarism and ferocity with which the nations had been want to carry on their destructive feuds." (Hegel's *Philosophy of History*, Chapter III)

Cyrus's philosophy influenced great historical figures, such as Karl Marx, Friedrich Nietzsche, Friedrich Engels, Jean-Paul Sartre, and more.

Cyrus the Great mostly ruled from Ecbatana until Pasargadae was built, but the empire had four capital cities. Xenophon goes on to specify the monarch's annual schedule. We cannot be sure this schedule applied to Cyrus, but it was in place by the time of Darius I. Babylon had a warm and sunny climate, and the king ruled from there for seven months of the year. During spring, he would rule from Susa for around three months. During the heat of mid-summer, he would rule from Ecbatana in the Median Highlands, where the climate was tolerable and cooler. Pasargadae, the ceremonial capital, was a place of vision and comfort for Cyrus, where he had his famous gardens with trees and plants from all across the empire. Here, he spent time with his family in his private palace. Pasargadae remained a sacred place even after it was replaced with Persepolis in the time of Darius I. All the Achaemenid kings were crowned at Pasargadae.

Intelligence Services

To ensure each satrapy functioned in accordance with the rules and regulations of the empire, Cyrus created special positions for monitoring the provinces. These men were specialized agents of the "King of Kings." During the time of Darius I, they could make unannounced inspections in the provinces.

The "Eye of the King" served as an extension of the king's purview. They watched the satraps and were an almost covert extension of the monarch, as he wished to have knowledge of what happened behind his back. To put it more bluntly, they were the king's spies. Both Xenophon and Ctesias emphasized the power wielded by the Eye of the King. They enabled the king to have firsthand knowledge of his subjects. In Cyrus's time, it was done for justice and fairness, but afterward, it became corrupted. Xenophon, who was born long after Cyrus died, wrote about seeing people on the roads as he traveled through the Persian Empire who had lost their eyes due to committing a crime against the king. In Ctesias's *Persica*, he mentions Persians gouging out eyes as punishment for treason.

The "Ears of the King" would listen for any rumors and investigate and confirm findings before reporting directly to the king. This included corruption, mismanagement, theft, and satraps who had abused their power.

The king's secretaries held independent positions and were seen as the most important authorities besides the King of Kings. They had a direct line of communication with the king. Functioning as a monitor, the secretary's role included checking on the administration, tax collection, and law and order in their provinces. They were seen as the king's closest and most trusted confidants. The responsibility of reading the king's private letters to the satraps also fell to the king's secretaries.

An example of how this position functioned comes to us via Herodotus, who describes an instance of Darius the Great's use of a secretary; yet again, we do not know if it was the same in the time of Cyrus II. Oroetes (also called Oroetus in some translations), the satrap in charge of Phrygia, Lydia, and Ionia during the rule of Darius I, had a personal army of one thousand soldiers. When the king's secretary read out instructions for the one thousand soldiers to cease protecting Oroetes and execute him, they immediately obeyed.

The Achaemenid Empire was advanced, successful, innovative, and ruled by a centralized bureaucratic government that built an unequaled infrastructure. According to some ancient accounts, the framework of what Cyrus initiated and Darius refined was so efficient that after Alexander the Great conquered Persia, he made very few changes, if any.

The road system called the Royal Road, which went from Susa to Sardis, led to the innovative postal service by the time of Darius that served the whole empire. It was called Chapar Khaneh ("courier house"). Each Chapar Khaneh was a resting and resupply station along the Royal Road. Here, the *chapars* or couriers could switch to a fresh horse and get supplies for their journey. It only took the *chapars* seven days to travel from Sardis to Susa, whereas an ordinary traveler would take ninety days or more, according to Herodotus. They were thought to have traveled "twenty-four seven" (night and day, every day) in safe areas and in emergencies.

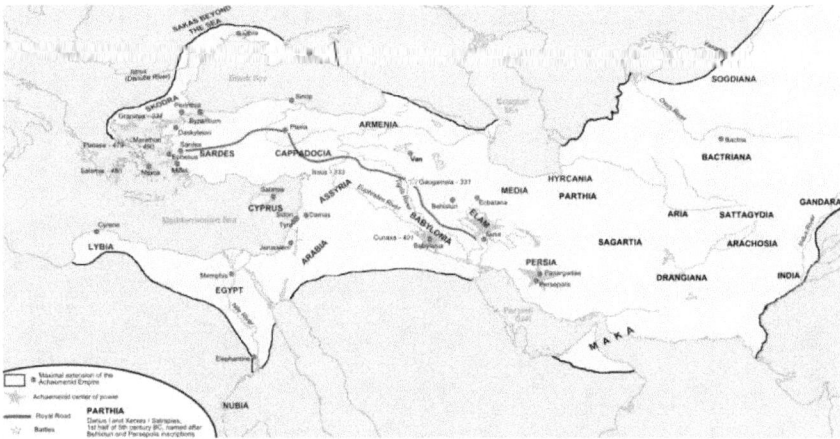

Map of the Achaemenid Empire with the Royal Road, which went from Susa in Elam to Sardis in Lydia.

Excavations in the 1930s uncovered over ten thousand fragments of cuneiform tablets that detailed the daily administration and transactions of the Persian Empire. The language is mostly Elamite, which has not been deciphered. Only one tablet in Old Persian—the brainchild of Darius—has been read and understood thus far. Personal and governmental seals and impressions were also found in what is known as the Persepolis Administrative Archives.

After the subjection of the whole of Mesopotamia and Iran, all written communication between provinces was in Official Aramaic or Imperial Aramaic. According to historians, this contributed greatly to the successful control of the vast empire.

Herodotus complimented these bureaucratic systems and stated they were well maintained and excellently served.

Chapter 7: Religious Tolerance

Diplomat Par Excellence

Cyrus the Great, the charismatic monarch of Persia, had a way with words. He was an excellent diplomat, yet it appears that his wisdom came from a deeper origin. It was as if his words echoed the true feelings, beliefs, and emotions in his heart. He spoke from his heart to his subjects, his administrators, his military, and his advisors. He was a genuinely great man who became a great ruler and, in the process, created a great empire.

Of course, we are aware that much of his words and deeds are embroidered with myths and legends by those who wrote about him years after his reign, but there are signs in the annals of conquered nations that he was admired by his friends and enemies.

Xenophon's account of Cyrus's advice to his sons, friends, and magistrates when he was on his deathbed almost makes one wish that we had a contemporary record of his sayings and advice. Something similar to Confucius's or Solomon's proverbs would be ideal, but for now, scholars have to be content with what records and secondhand sources exist.

The Achaemenid Empire was once home to 44 percent of the world's population, according to guestimates by some scholars. This multiethnic civilization was comprised of nations and tribes that spoke different languages, practiced diverse religions, wore different clothing, and had different cultural and societal frameworks and worldviews.

When Cyrus conquered these foreign territories, he must have thought deeply and sought input from his councilors on ideas of how to rule an empire that stretched such a large geographic area. We know he mostly left each region's system in place at the beginning while he figured it all out.

Perhaps his thought process was influenced by his childhood years, which were spent as the son of a cowherd playing with the sons of the nobles or elites. At the age of ten, his social status changed completely when he was sent to fill his real role as the son of the king of Anshan. Cyrus experienced the world from both sides, first as the son of a servant and then as the crown prince of a kingdom. His experiences in life must have influenced his personality and his attitude toward people at all levels of society.

And then he became a powerful but benevolent king. His subjects were from all classes and came from many different societies, different ethnicities, and diverse cultures. He had to find a way to rule, and he undoubtedly realized that if he acknowledged, respected, tolerated, and managed the diversity, he would rule from a place of strength and peace since he would not be faced with religious, cultural, and societal rebellions.

In practical terms, tolerance was the best way to keep the peace and for Persia to become a prosperous, harmonious, multicultural empire. Cyrus was unconventional in his approach to ruling at that time in history. His policies of respect and acceptance of the traditions, beliefs, and customs of his subjects secured the unification of his empire. He was a king like none before him. He was honored as the father of his people, even when his power was sometimes feared by the people he ruled.

After conquering Babylon, he presented himself as a liberator and the legitimate successor to the vanquished king rather than a conqueror. His words were followed by actions that supported his policy statement.

The conquest of Babylon played a significant role during King Cyrus's reign. It gave him control of the trade routes on the Silk Road, the road that linked Babylon to Ecbatana, and the road that linked Susa in Elam to Sardis in Anatolia. Later, the road between Susa and Sardis was turned into the well-constructed Royal Road by Darius I. At that point, it was even more valuable because the new road had grooves for wagons. Imagine the impact on trade and travel!

Having control of such a vast empire inspired Cyrus to have his vision for the empire inscribed onto a clay cylinder and placed in the foundations of the temple of Marduk, known as Esagila, in the city of Babylon.

According to some sources, both Alexander the Great and Julius Caesar were inspired by Cyrus.

Historians and scholars today postulate the policies of Cyrus the Great were based on the teachings of Zoroaster. Zoroastrians emphasize the freedom of choice between dark and light or good and evil by the individual. This choice, when followed by honorable deeds, good thoughts, and good words of the individual, will increase the *aša* in the world and in the person. *Aša* refers to the "good working" or "good order" of the world.

Cyrus's ideology and the strategies he used to rule the empire formed the central thread through which he prevented rebellion and received cooperation from servants up to the highest of elite classes. His policies of respect and freedom when it came to religion, customs, and social structures ensured the smooth running of the administration. The government was efficient and functional on all levels while he was alive.

King Cyrus declared himself the guardian of temples and sanctuaries of all the religions across the empire. He allowed customs and traditions to continue without interruption after conquered nations became part of the Persian Empire. At times, he even participated in local ceremonies and rituals. The nobles and priests of new regions became a part of his framework, and he granted regions limited political autonomy. This was usually done as part of a larger strategy. So, for example, allowing the Jewish people to return to Judea helped him create a boundary between the Persian Empire and Egypt.

An interesting fact regarding the Persian Empire is that religious tolerance and the role of women in society were innovative and visionary. Clay tablets excavated in Persepolis, the ceremonial capital started by Darius, detail the position of women in society, business, and finance. Texts detail financial transactions between women who traveled for personal reasons or conducting business.

These texts date back to the rule of Artaxerxes I (465–424 BCE) and record a considerable number of transactions.

Snapshot of Equality

To understand the extent of the equality of women in the Persian Empire, we must delve deeper into the exact role women played in business, culture, and society.

Ancient Persian women were basically considered equal in status to men. Owning land, running a business, traveling, and getting equal pay for work were basic rights for Persian women. Royal women were allowed to have their own council meetings to discuss policies, and their opinions mattered. Cyrus ensured women of different classes were treated with dignity and respect.

Women's rights fluctuated throughout the ages. Their independence drastically deteriorated much later, especially from the 1ˢᵗ millennium CE, often due to religious beliefs, including those of the Abrahamic faiths. Views that women are inherently sinful, incapable of deciding their own fate, and need to be controlled under the veil of protection are present in correspondence between Christian church fathers. This is essentially a lapse in civilizations' progress that has lasted up to the present day and is legally still entrenched in the policies of certain countries.

Although the Achaemenid Empire was a patriarchal system, women had rights. A female hierarchy later formed an essential framework within the Persian Empire.

Mother of the King

Mother of the King's Heir (Principal Wife)

King's Daughters

King's Sisters

King's Lesser Wives

Council Women

Noble Women

Wives & Relatives of Courtiers

Wives of Satraps

Wives of Military Men

Military Women

Business women

Laborers

Servants & Slaves

Concubines

Illigitimate Daughters

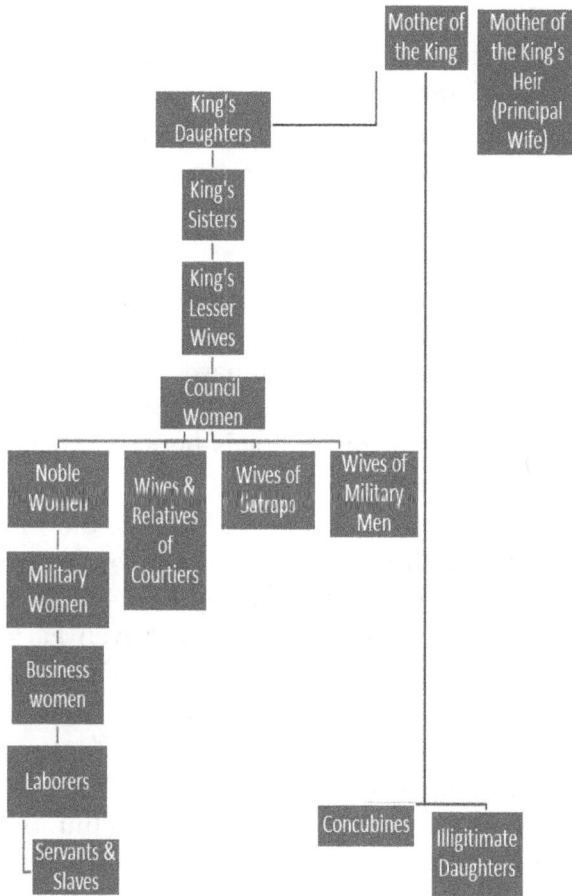

Hierarchy of women.

Key Roles of Women

Mother of the King and the Principal Wife

The king's mother and the principal wife, also called Shahbanu or "King's Lady," traveled with the king on military campaigns, like Cambyses II's wife, Roxane, who was killed in Nubia while traveling with him on a military campaign. They were accompanied by their own attendants, had places of honor at banquets, held their own courts, signed treaties and agreements with their own seals, and had unlimited access to the king. We know from the Book of Esther in the Christian Bible that this had changed by the time of Esther, who replaced Vashti as the wife of the Persian king, Xerxes I or Ahasuerus in the Torah.

Women could choose whom they wanted to marry, although treaties, alliances, and business transactions were secured with marriages to the king's daughters and sisters.

Women in the Military

Excavations have confirmed that some women were warriors in the Achaemenid Empire. We again do not know if this happened during Cyrus's rule. It may very well have been the case, though, as the women warrior tribes of the steppes had contact with Cyrus in the past and were part of his people's heritage when the Persians moved to Iran centuries before Cyrus.

Xerxes I was so impressed with the skills of the woman warrior Artemisia I of Caria that she was honored by being escorted to safety by his sons after the Battle of Salamis in 480 BCE. According to reports from a scholar by the name of Kaveh Farrokh, "tombs attesting to the existence of Iranian-speaking women warriors have [been found in Iran and] also been excavated in Eastern Europe."

Pantea Arteshbod, in conjunction with her husband, organized the elite Immortals under Cyrus the Great. Artunis (540–500 BCE) was a skilled lieutenant commander of the Immortals. Persian women warriors fought in the Persian armies throughout the Achaemenid period, such as Youtab Aryobarzan (d. 330 BCE), who was among those who defended the Persian Gate. Youtab Aryobarzan had great courage and skill and is said to have died alongside her brother, Ariobarzanes (330 BCE), during the Battle of the Persian Gate during Alexander the Great's conquest of the Persian Empire.

Women in Business

Women conducted business, as can be seen in texts excavated in Persepolis. Irdabama was a businesswoman, probably during the reign of Darius, who personally managed trade and production in Iran, Babylonia, Egypt, Media, and Syria. She oversaw around 480 laborers, excluding her extensive number of personal attendants.

Laborers, Servants, and Slaves

Women and men worked side by side, and women were often supervisors and managers. Female supervisors were known as *arashshara*. They were well paid and given a larger amount of grain and wine as overseers of a large number of subordinates.

Wages were based on skill, experience, and the type of job. There was no difference in wages based on gender. Pregnant women were actually paid higher wages. New mothers received higher wages for the first month after the birth of their child. The physician, mother, and midwife received an additional amount if the child was a boy.

Slaves throughout Persia were treated more like servants and earned a wage. Laws under Darius I stated that no slave could be mistreated or killed. A slaveowner who disobeyed this law would be judged according to the crime, and a slave would be viewed in the same light as a free citizen.

Religions in Cyrus's Empire

Depiction of the chief god of Babylon, Marduk, on a cylinder seal from the 9ᵗʰ century BCE.

https://commons.wikimedia.org/wiki/File:Marduk_and_pet.jpg

Proto-Indo-Iranian Pantheons

The nomadic tribes that inhabited the area around the Zagros Mountains and the Elamites worshiped a pantheon of gods. These nomadic tribes were also referred to as Proto-Indo-Europeans and wandered the steppes of the region. The Proto-Indo-Iranians were an offshoot of these Indo-European nomads, and they mixed with Semitic and other people groups as they moved. They may even be linked to an extinct Anatolian branch of civilization and appear to date to around 1900 BCE.

The pantheon of gods may have matured in the Cradle of Civilization (Mesopotamia), but we are aware of many earlier gods, such as the mother goddess represented in almost every ancient culture. When we compare the pantheons of Greek, Roman, Celtic, and Scandinavian peoples, there are similarities in the myths and powers of the gods. The religious concepts were essentially the same or similar, but the names were different. For example, the Sky Father morphed into Zeus in Greek mythology and was called Jupiter in the Roman pantheon.

According to Xenophon, Cyrus made vows to the god Mithra. Mithra was associated with light, the sun, justice, oaths, and covenants. Mithra was the all-seeing god that protected the harvest, guarded livestock, and reigned over the waters. Texts that have been deciphered have led scholars to believe Cyrus followed a polytheistic belief system; however, other scholars and historians are certain that he was a Zoroastrian.

Nevertheless, we can be certain there was a plethora of deities across his empire. Cyrus certainly must have done his homework because, by all accounts, he made offerings to each town's patron deities when he visited there.

The ancient pantheons from the earliest records and excavations had gods that ruled all aspects of life and origins. However, we do not fully know or can interpret all of the gods yet. A case in point is the new findings in Anatolia over the past few decades, such as Göbekli Tepe. Most pantheons usually included a god of the sky, a dawn deity, a fertility or mother earth goddess, a weather or thunder god, and a water god.

Sky Father

The Sky Father was the supreme deity of the Proto-Indo-European pantheon, according to verbal accounts. Dyeus, the Sky Father, has similar powers as Zeus (Greek) and Jupiter (Roman). Tiwaz, a Germanic god (Tyr in Old Norse), wielded the same power and influence over the elements. When translated directly, Dyeus means "daylight-sky god." Dyeus was noted as having a relationship with the Earth Mother.

The Dawn Goddess

Mallory and Adams, who edited the *Encyclopedia of Indo-European Culture* in 1997, reconstructed the name of the Dawn Goddess to *hausos*, meaning "dawn," and other texts refer to her as *dhughtēr diwos*, meaning "daughter of the sky god." The evidence supporting their work can be found in the Vedas and a poem by

Homer. Mallory is an expert in archaeology, and Adams is a distinguished linguist.

The Dawn Goddess drove the night away and was revered as an important deity, as can be seen in preserved texts from ancient Indo-European languages.

Mother Earth

Information about the Mother Earth deity remains controversial to this day, as some evidence refers to Mother Earth not as a goddess but as the earth itself. The translated meaning of her name is "broad earth." According to other uncovered evidence, she is revered as the wife of the sky god. In Greek, Gaia is the personification of the earth as a goddess, and in the Roman pantheon, this goddess is called Tellus Mater.

Regardless of the controversies, the Mother Earth goddess illustrates the ancient thought processes. People wondered about the things around them that were inexplicable, like the process of childbirth. Childbirth is similar to the earth sprouting new life in the spring.

The Thunderer

When directly translated, the name Perkwunos or *perk'unos* means "The Striker" or "The Lord of Oaks." This deity rules over the weather, and his name is invoked during times of drought. In Indo-European mythology, the god of thunder battles a multi-headed water serpent so the serpent will release the water it has been holding. Perkwunos's weapon is referred to as meld-n, which linguists interpret as being either a hammer or a lightning bolt.

The Nephew of Waters

The name of this god appears to be Apạm Napāt in Zoroastrianism, which has been translated as son, grandson, or nephew by various scholars of Indo-Iranian cultures. Evidence of this god is only found in Indo-Iranian accounts, and he does not have a Roman or Greek counterpart. Neptune is the Roman god of freshwater and seawater, and the Greek god Poseidon would be the equivalent god to Neptune. However, there is no "nephew" god, at least according to linguists who have examined Greek, Roman, Old Irish, and Latin texts.

There is little or no evidence left of the other gods or goddesses of the Proto-Indo-European pantheon. Even the creation story of the Proto-Indo-European civilization is fragmented, as written accounts are scarce or nonexistent. Excavations in Turkey during this century have pushed back the timeline of religious ceremonial centers to the centuries following the last ice age. Scholars do not yet understand how to interpret and understand the magnificent etchings and carvings discovered at these centers, but they are fairly certain that most were done in honor of one or more deities.

Zoroastrianism

Xenophon's *Cyropaedia* is filled with accounts regarding the beliefs, life, and religious tolerance of Cyrus the Great. He goes further by saying the policies of king Cyrus were "based on a respect for individual people, ethnic groups, other religions, and ancient kingdoms."

The *Cyropaedia* extols the virtues of an ideal ruler, which Xenophon sees personified in Cyrus the Great. "What other man but Cyrus, after having overturned an empire, ever died with the title of their father from the people whom he had brought under his power? For it is plain that this is a name for one that bestows, rather than for one that takes away."

There are plenty of indications that Cyrus followed the teachings of Zoroastrianism, although there is no conclusive proof of that. In addition, he called on Mithra instead of Ahura Mazda in an account by Xenophon. In the *Histories* by Herodotus, he stresses that Cyrus was referred to as father by his subjects. He was a fair, kind, uncorrupt, and charismatic ruler.

Cyrus and the Jews

The Hebrew Bible mentions the Persian king as the "anointed one" who liberated the Jewish people from slavery in Babylon. The Old Testament of the Bible mentions King Cyrus over twenty-three times in the books of Ezra, Chronicles, Daniel, and Isaiah.

King Nebuchadnezzar II invaded Judea and conquered Jerusalem in 597 BCE. He enslaved some of the Jewish people and exiled the king of Judah and the people he captured to Babylon.

The next attack on Jerusalem in 586 BCE is described in the Old Testament:

"He burned the house of the Lord, the king's house, and all the houses of Jerusalem; every great house he burned down. All the army of the Chaldeans who were with the captain of the guard broke down the walls around Jerusalem. Nebuzaradan the captain of the guard carried into exile the rest of the people who were left in the city and the deserters who had defected to the king of Babylon – all the rest of the population. But the captain of the guard left some of the poorest people of the land to be vinedressers and tillers of the soil." (2 Kings 25:9-12)

These events resulted in what is called the Babylonian captivity. What was almost worse for the Jewish people was that Nebuchadnezzar destroyed Solomon's Temple and took everything in it, including the sacred objects that validated their faith, to Babylon's treasury.

While enslaved in Babylon, the Jewish people were persecuted by their masters and the rest of the Babylonian citizens. Initially, they tried to continue to worship God, but this resulted in severe beatings and punishment, at times even death. The priests redacted, changed, and transcribed ancient texts to influence and keep Judaism alive. For instance, Abraham came from "Ur of the Chaldeans" because the Chaldeans and their lands would be understood by the Jewish people. The ancient inhabitants of that land in Abraham's time, including the Sumerians of Ur and other Mesopotamian peoples, were long gone by the time of the Babylonian captivity.

Cyrus is mentioned in the Christian Old Testament in the Book of Isaiah, Chapter 45, where he is referred to as the Lord's "anointed" one. "He is my shepherd, and he shall carry out all my purpose, and who says of Jerusalem, it shall be rebuilt, and of the temple, your foundation shall be laid. Thus says the Lord to his anointed, to Cyrus, whose right hand I have grasped to subdue nations before him and strip kings of their robes, to open doors before him and the gates shall not be closed."

After Cyrus conquered Babylon in 539 BCE, the Jewish people who were enslaved in the city welcomed King Cyrus as their liberator. Cyrus decreed the Jewish people were free to return to their homeland. In the Old Testament Book of Ezra, it is recorded that 42,360 Jews returned to Jerusalem and Judah, excluding their servants and handmaids.

Cyrus the Great also instructed the Jews to rebuild the Temple in Jerusalem and provided finances for this project. The project was completed during the reign of King Darius I, who also provided funds for the Temple's reconstruction. King Cyrus also issued orders that all items of value that had been taken by the Babylonians were to be returned to them and the Temple.

Some of the Jewish people remained in Babylon, where, over the decades, they started businesses and had families that often included Babylonians. The Jews who remained in Babylon were given the freedom to practice their religion and were left unhindered during times of worship or religious festivals.

Reliable Proof of the Babylonian Invasion

Recent archaeological discoveries prove, without a doubt, that the Babylonians invaded Judah and destroyed their cities. Jewish chronicles and prophets also recorded the events that happened.

Geomagnetic fields throughout Israel have enabled researchers from Tel Aviv University (TAU) and the Hebrew University of Jerusalem (HU) to form a clearer understanding and provide physical evidence of the Babylonian attacks and conquests of Israel and Judah.

In 2020, researchers reconstructed the magnetic field on the day the First Temple and the city of Jerusalem were invaded by Nebuchadnezzar and the mighty Babylonian army. The date was the ninth of Av, 586 BCE. This date has become a traditional day of mourning for the Jewish people, during which they remember the destruction of the First Temple in Jerusalem, which was built by King Solomon. Av is a month in the Jewish calendar. According to the Gregorian calendar, Av takes place in July and August. The start and end dates of Av vary, but the days always fall across both months.

Using items recovered at archaeological sites across the region, geophysicists have tracked magnetic minerals that recorded the magnetic field at the time of the conflagration. They tested the new dating method at several ancient sites where the results could be compared to already confirmed dates. The destruction of Jerusalem by Nebuchadnezzar II was confirmed to have happened on the ninth of Av. They also proved archaeologists' theories that the Babylonians did not destroy all the Judean cities and towns during this invasion.

Scientific Breakthrough of the Century

This new method of dating will help archaeologists determine the age of findings at excavation sites by using geomagnetic data.

Twenty researchers from different countries and disciplines accurately dated twenty-one layers of destruction that occurred in seventeen archaeological sites in Israel. The destruction of the Kingdom of Judah was one of the most interesting date confirmations exposed by this new method of dating.

Chapter 8: The Cyrus Cylinder

What Is the Cyrus Cylinder?

The Cyrus Cylinder is made of clay. It resembles a small barrel. The clay was applied and baked in stages around a core of large grey stones. The cylinder was thus built up in layers and baked numerous times until its final shape and size were achieved. Once this was done, a fine slip of clay was added to be used as the surface for the inscription.

The Cyrus Cylinder was used to describe King Cyrus, his exploits, his conquests, his building projects, and his magnanimity toward the people and places he conquered.

The inscription praises Cyrus and details his lineage, stating that he was a descendant of an age-old line of kings and that he had defeated the common-born king of Babylon, Nabonidus, who was an oppressor of the people. According to the text, the chief Babylonian god, Marduk, had chosen Cyrus to restore peace and prosperity to the Babylonians. The text also asks for blessings from the god Marduk for Cyrus and his son Cambyses. The cylinder refers to King Ashurbanipal, who restored the walls previously during the Assyrian occupation and who left a similar inscription, which was found while restoring the city wall of Babylon. It continues by praising Cyrus as being a generous king to the citizens of Babylon and for rebuilding temples and cult sanctuaries across Mesopotamia and the empire. The text concludes by describing the restoration of Babylon's city wall.

The Cyrus Cylinder.

Prioryman, CC BY-SA 3.0 <https://creativecommons.org/licenses/by-sa/3.0>, via Wikimedia Commons; https://commons.wikimedia.org/wiki/File:Cyrus_Cylinder_front.jpg

During the original excavations in 1879 under the auspices of the British Museum, the cylinder broke into fragments. The section known as Fragment A was sent to the British Museum in London.

Fragment B was acquired by James B. Nies from Yale University from an antiquities dealer. Nies published the inscription in 1920. Fragment B could have been among the rubble left behind by the archaeologists, or it could have been removed during the original excavation. Fragment B was not identified as being part of the original Cyrus Cylinder until 1970 when Paul-Richard Berger of the University of Munster definitively confirmed its origin.

The script used on the baked cylinder is cuneiform, and the language of the text is Akkadian. It can be dated to around 539 BCE.

What Was Its Use

The Cyrus Cylinder was used as part of the foundational deposit of the temple of Marduk, known as the Esagila, in ancient Babylon. Foundation deposits are lined pits or holes under specific points of important buildings. These pits were filled with ceremonial objects and often included a clay tablet that chronicled the story of the person or building or why the tablet was placed there. These ceremonial objects were believed to ensure the building's divine protection and prevent it from falling into ruin.

These foundation deposits also typically described a ruler's legacy and provided future rulers with an account of the conquests and virtues of the builders of the temple or other important buildings.

However, the Cyrus Cylinder has proved to be much more important than the usual foundation deposit. Modern-day Iran adopted the cylinder as the national symbol of Iran by Shah Mohammad Reza of the Pahlavi family. In 1971, the Cyrus Cylinder went on display in Tehran to commemorate the 2,500-year celebration of the Persian Empire; it was on loan from the British Museum.

A replica of the Cyrus Cylinder was presented to the United Nations Secretary General at the time, U Thant, by Princess Ashraf Pahlavi. According to Princess Ashraf, "the heritage of Cyrus was the heritage of human understanding, tolerance, courage, compassion, and, above all, human liberty." She added that her brother, the shah of Persia (now Iran), Mohammad Reza Pahlavi, saw the Cyrus Cylinder as a "charter of human rights."

There are scholars who suggest the wording on the cylinder follows the usual pattern of a declaration, something most ancient rulers did at the beginning of their rule. In their eyes, the cylinder is propaganda. But in the case of Cyrus, there is proof from contemporary sources that his deeds matched his words. The best example here is the Jewish people who were allowed to return to their homeland. Cyrus was also respected and admired by his enemies, which would indicate that the words on the cylinder had at least some truth to them.

Why Is It Important

Neil MacGregor, former director of the British Museum, occasionally said the importance of the Cyrus Cylinder is that it represents "the first attempt we know about running a society, a state, with different nationalities and faiths—a new kind of statecraft." He is seen as the foremost expert on the subject of the Cyrus Cylinder.

Biblical scholars have traditionally seen the inscriptions on the cylinder as proof of biblical authenticity regarding the Jews' return to Jerusalem to rebuild the temple that Nebuchadnezzar had destroyed. The edict of Cyrus that allowed the Jewish people and other exiles to return home after being held captive in Babylon was issued after he captured the city of Babylon. This is told in the Book of Ezra, which states, "Then the family heads of Judah and Benjamin, and the priests and Levites—everyone whose heart God had moved—prepared to go up and build the house of the Lord in Jerusalem. All their neighbors assisted them with articles of silver and gold, with goods and livestock, and with valuable gifts, in addition to all the freewill offerings" (Ezra 1:6-11).

The biblical interpretation has been refuted by numerous other academics, as the text in some translations only refers to people from Mesopotamia and does not specify any one people group in particular.

In Shah Mohammad Reza Pahlavi's book, published in 1967, titled *The White Revolution*, he refers to the Cyrus Cylinder as the "first declaration of human rights." The shah describes Cyrus the Great as an advocate for humane principles, justice, and liberty, things that are all stated on the Cyrus Cylinder. He continues by saying that Cyrus was the first ruler to allow his subjects "freedom of opinion and other basic rights."

In 1968, the United Nations held a human rights conference in Tehran, which was opened by the shah, the last ruler of Iran before it became a strictly Muslim country. In his opening address, the shah said the text as written on the Cyrus Cylinder was the predecessor of what we refer to as the Universal Declaration of Human Rights.

It is interesting to note that several of the Founding Fathers and signatories of the Declaration of Independence of the United States of America are known to have had copies of Xenophon's *Cyropaedia*, which they treasured. It is said Thomas Jefferson had three copies! The Declaration of Independence is echoed in the UN Charter of Human Rights and seeks to guarantee basic and equal human rights for all people in the world, something that is astonishingly similar to Cyrus the Great's vision as stated in the cuneiform text on the Cyrus Cylinder.

Shah Mohammad Reza Pahlavi stated in a Nowruz (New Year) address that 1971 would become known as the Cyrus the Great

Year. The year would be dedicated to the celebration of the anniversary of the Achaemenid Empire and Cyrus the Great. The shah hoped civilization would recognize the Persian Empire's contributions to society, business, and humanity. He stated in speeches that the Achaemenid era was a moment from Iran's national past that would serve as a model for the modern imperial society he hoped to create.

During that year, the Cyrus Cylinder and the official crest of Iran became a worldwide symbol. Magazines and journals published articles about the ancient Persian Empire. The British Museum loaned the original Cyrus Cylinder to Iran for the duration of the festivities. The cylinder was displayed at the Shahyad Tower, now renamed the Azadi Tower, in Tehran.

The official celebrations began on October 12th, 1971, and ended a week later in a spectacular ceremony at the tomb of Cyrus in Pasargadae. The date of October 12th coincides with the day Cyrus is believed to have entered Babylon in 539 BCE.

Where Is It Today?

The excavations of the temple of Marduk in Babylon, where the cylinder was found, were done on behalf of the trustees of the British Museum and with a decree from the Ottoman Sultan, Abdul Hamid I, which stated that antiquities found at the site could be removed, packed, and sent to England, provided there were no duplicates. To ensure these instructions were followed, a representative of the sultan was on hand to examine all objects as they were uncovered.

The Cyrus Cylinder was dispatched to the British Museum in London after its excavation in March 1879 by Assyriologist and archaeologist Hormuzd Rassam, who had taken over from the original excavator, Austen Henry Layard, who also taught and trained him. Rassam was trained further in London to become the first-known Middle Eastern archaeologist.

Fragment A and Fragment B were reunited in 1972 after Yale gave Fragment B to the British Museum on a permanent loan in return for the loan of a similar clay tablet. The Cyrus Cylinder remains in the British Museum in London to this day and has only been loaned out for exhibitions four times.

This ancient declaration of human rights is continuously used as a symbol by the United Nations. A replica of the Cyrus Cylinder can be seen at the United Nations Headquarters in New York City.

Archaeological Value

The archaeological information that can be gathered from the Cyrus Cylinder is invaluable, as it gives details on the cities and towns invaded by King Cyrus and the timelines of these conquests. Additionally, the information on the cylinder also corresponds with the information in the Bible, specifically in the books of Isaiah, Ezra, and Chronicles. It basically confirms that in 539 BCE, the Persian conqueror Cyrus the Great allowed the Jewish people to be freed from captivity in Babylon.

Information from the Cyrus Cylinder tells us exactly how the city was conquered. On October 12th on the Julian Calendar (October 7th on the Gregorian Calendar) in 539 BCE, the Achaemenid army entered the gates of Babylon without any resistance from the inhabitants, including the army. Cyrus the Great entered the city on October 29th. He was welcomed by the citizens as a liberator and proclaimed himself "king of Babylon, king of Sumer and Akkad, king of the four corners (or quarters) of the world."

An important text on the Cyrus Cylinder describes the conquest of Babylon and that his army peacefully marched into the city as liberators. This claim is supported by a statement inscribed in the Chronicle of Nabonidus. Nabonidus was the last king of Babylon. He was considered an evil tyrant who offended the city god Marduk and forced his foreign religious ideas upon his subjects by honoring the moon god Sin. Myth has it that his disrespect for the patron deity of Babylon caused Marduk to intervene and summon Cyrus to rectify the abominations in Babylon. Cyrus is considered to be chosen by the supreme god.

The Cyrus Cylinder remained under the walls of the Esagila, the temple of the patron god Marduk, until it was rediscovered in 1879. Placing this cylinder as a foundation deposit continued a centuries-long Mesopotamian tradition. Cyrus honored this tradition, as he did the sacred customs of every society that he conquered.

The archaeological value of the Cyrus Cylinder is based on its three main decrees:

1. A formally stated political declaration of racial, religious, and linguistic equality, which includes formerly displaced, enslaved, and deported peoples. They were allowed to return home and restore their destroyed temples.

2. Further text detailing the respect Cyrus had for humanity, freedom, and the humane treatment of all people, regardless of their origins or religious beliefs.

3. Cyrus the Great's commitment, which was to turn the empire into a prosperous, peaceful, innovative, and harmonious empire of nations that traded and shared with each other and the rest of the world.

Chapter 9: Death and Burial

Unless we believe that Cyrus's tomb is empty or contains his headless remains, we have to consider Xenophon's version of his death. Xenophon states that Cyrus died at a ripe old age in his bed in his palace in Pasargadae. As a righteous man who always honored Ahura Mazda and the other gods of his subjects when in their regions, Cyrus was warned by the gods that his end was near. He was tired and happy to face death because, as a Zoroastrian, he believed that only the body died; the soul went on. He had time to put his affairs in order.

Cyrus called his two sons, who had accompanied him to Pasargadae from Babylon, and his friends and some magistrates to his bedside, where he was resting. He appointed his son Cambyses in his place as king of kings and his son Tanyoxarces as ruler of the satraps of Media, Armenia, and Cadusia. He advised them to always honor and support each other and to have each other's backs at all times against conspiracies. He said the key to successfully ruling over such a large empire was to make others your fellow guardians of territories. After what seemed an enormously long speech for such a tired old man, passing out instructions and advice to all present, Cyrus pulled the covers over his head and passed away.

According to Ctesias, Cyrus was mortally wounded in a battle against the Derbices, a familial clan of the Massagetae nomadic tribe in the northeast of Iran. He lingered for three days, during which time he put his affairs in order before dying. His troops brought his body home to Pasargadae. According to Strabo, the Greek geographer, philosopher, and historian (63 BCE–23 CE), Cyrus died in a battle against the Scythians. According to Berossus, a Babylonian scribe and astrologer who wrote a history of Babylonia (c. 310 BCE), Cyrus died in battle against the Dahae, another Scythian-linked tribe.

It is clear that many different legends were repeated by many ancient scribes and would-be historians. Folktales and the passing of time, along with migrations and replacements of tribes and peoples, further confused the issue. Despite Herodotus's embroidered histories, his version of Cyrus's death remains perhaps the most popular and is well worth repeating.

Herodotus's *Histories* Version

Herodotus believed the Caucasus Mountains to be the highest of all the mountain ranges. To the east of the mountains lay the Caspian Sea. Bordering the Caspian Sea and stretching far to the east from there lay a very large plain. The strongest tribe dwelling there was the Massagetae.

Again, according to Herodotus, the Massagetae were akin to the Scythians in dress, except for their distinctive pointed caps. They also shared many other similar customs. Unlike the Scythians, though, Herodotus says there were stories that the Massagetae ate their men folk once they got old. Only those who died from an illness were buried. Maybe that is why Herodotus did not visit this region in his travels. Herodotus also mentions they had a strange custom where women could sleep around after marriage but not the men.

The Massagetae were often confused with the Scythians. They are still referred to as one of the Scythian tribes, the Saka, or at least as relatives of the Saka. Recent studies have indicated the tribal links across the Eurasian steppe, from the Balkans eastward, were often intertwined and genetically linked with Indo-European and Indo-Iranian peoples.

One of the outstanding qualities of the Massagetae was their horsemanship. They may even have had a cult centered around horses since they sacrificed horses to their gods. These nomadic warrior people may have had settlements at cult centers. Scholars hypothesize this due to their extensive use of metals and bronzemaking, which means they surely must have had permanent facilities for the process of smelting and making metal alloys.

Herodotus says they only worshiped one deity, their sun god. Mounted on fleet horses, the Massagetae often raided towns and cities of neighboring kingdoms and states and got away with it. In 530 BCE, Cyrus wanted to safeguard his eastern borders against the incursions by the nomadic peoples of the steppe. The king of the Massagetae had died, and his wife, Queen Tomyris, inherited the throne. In other versions, Tomyris was the only child of the overlord of several tribes. She was raised to take over. She married a king from another tribe but was already queen over all the tribes when this happened.

Cyrus thought the change in leadership was an excellent opportunity to gain control of the steppes and their gold and bronze. The Massagetae used gold and bronze in everything, including armor and weapons. Even horse bits contained portions of bronze and gold.

Queen Tomyris was a warrior princess who then became a warrior queen. Legends couple the Massagetae with the famous Amazon warrior women described by the ancient Greek authors. It is likely that, instead of the tribes consisting of only women, they were tribes with equal standing, joint duties, and the training of both men and women from an early age.

An interesting tomb containing four women was discovered in 2019 on the River Don in Russia, which seems to confirm the Greek legends of these fighting women. They were of different ages; there was a teenager, two young women, and a forty-five to fifty-year-old woman. They were buried at the same time. This burial confirmed the warrior status of women. It contained various types of weapons, such as spears, knives, and arrowheads, as well as jewelry. The crowning glory of the find was arguably the magnificent headdress, called a calathus, on the head of the older woman—the first to be found in situ.

Testing the Waters

Cyrus sent a delegation to Tomyris with gifts and a letter asking for her hand in marriage. The astute Tomyris knew that he was after her kingdom rather than her. She refused to accept his proposal. Cyrus realized his ploy was not going to work and that he would have to engage in battle with the Massagetae if his heart was set on conquering the steppes. This led to Cyrus himself leading the Persians in his quest.

When Cyrus and his vast army arrived at the Araxes River bordering his empire, he tasked his engineers and troops with building a bridge to safely cross the river with their cavalry and carts loaded with their equipment, tools, tents, food, and weapons. Tomyris sent him a message suggesting in no uncertain terms that he should stay in his empire and leave her and her people in peace. She added that if he insisted on testing the strength of the Massagetae, there were two options. Either Cyrus should let her ride back from the border to give him time to cross into her territory, or he could withdraw the same distance and leave her army to invade his territory.

As was his habit, Cyrus called together his advisors. Most agreed that it was better for them to withdraw and allow the Massagetae to cross since they could choose a battlefield and set up their troops in ideal formations. Wise old Croesus, though, disagreed. He reminded Cyrus that he and his men were not immortal. If the Massagetae should enter his realm and win a battle, they would not stop there but go on to conquer his provinces. Cyrus could lose his empire. If, on the other hand, Cyrus should attack the Massagetae in their own territory, he could lay an ambush to trap them and gain victory.

Croesus's plan was that they should cross the river, then set up their camp with a scrumptious feast laid out with all sorts of foods and lots of wine. The main Persian forces would withdraw to the river, leaving only a small force of decrepit soldiers at the feast. The Massagetae would attack the camp, easily overcome these men, and then undoubtedly be tempted to celebrate their victory by carrying on with the feasting and drinking. Once they were drunk and incapacitated, the main Persian force could attack and capture them.

Croesus's plan sounded solid, and Cyrus went with it. Everything happened as Croesus had predicted. When the Massagetae were thoroughly drunk, the main Persian army attacked. Amongst their captives was Tomyris's son. Tomyris was livid. She sent a message to Cyrus saying there would be no retribution if he gave her son back unharmed, even though he was the victim of deceit and not beaten in an open and honest battle. However, if her son was harmed and Cyrus was set on continuing the war, she would drench him in more blood than he could ever want.

Meanwhile, Tomyris's son had revived from his drunken stupor. He begged Cyrus to set him free. The moment he was freed, he committed suicide because of his shame. There was no going back for Cyrus. The war would have to continue. The battle was fought with cavalry and foot soldiers, and this time, the Massagetae were the victors. Cyrus was among the casualties.

Queen Tomyris receiving the head of Cyrus.
https://commons.wikimedia.org/wiki/File:Queen_Tomyris_and_the_head_of_Cyrus_the_Great.jpg

Herodotus tells us that Tomyris collected a sack of human blood. She searched for Cyrus's body among the dead and stuck his head in the bag full of blood, just as she had threatened in her final message. In another version, her soldiers chopped off Cyrus's head after the battle and brought it to her. She then dunked it in blood.

The Tomb in Pasargadae

Cyrus's body was brought back to Pasargadae to the tomb that he had designed. There are no extant records of the trip or the burial ceremony. We can only imagine when and how the body of the beloved King of Kings was transported back to his city and laid to rest in his tomb. What we do know from Xenophon's descriptions of Cyrus's lifestyle is that he likely did not desire a grand ceremony. We can assume there were lots of mourning and burial rituals that had to be adhered to. Cyrus believed, at least according to Xenophon, that the body was merely a vessel for the soul, which carried on in the afterlife with intelligence while being unencumbered by the trappings of earthly life.

Alexander the Great, who greatly admired Cyrus's history and is said to have been inspired by him, entered the tomb when he and his troops conquered the Persians two centuries later. The ancient author known as Arrian (born c. 90 CE), in his work *The Anabasis of Alexander,* quotes a description from Aristobulus, a companion of Alexander, that they found the tomb damaged and broken into. Alexander was upset and gave Aristobulus instructions to restore the tomb.

Tomb of King Cyrus in Pasargadae.
Truth Seeker, CC BY-SA 3.0 <https://creativecommons.org/licenses/by-sa/3.0>, via Wikimedia Commons; https://commons.wikimedia.org/w/index.php?curid=14482534

The inside of the tomb had been greatly damaged and robbed. The lid of Cyrus's coffin had been broken, and pieces had been chopped off to remove it from the tomb, but the robbers were unable to get it out since the door was too small. At the time of Alexander, the burial chamber contained a divan and a table with Cyrus's gold-covered coffin. The divan had feet of gold, and on it was an array of richly colored clothes, jewelry, and weapons. The robbers had made off with anything else the tomb may have held. The remains of the skeleton were in disarray on the floor.

Chapter 10: The Legacy of Cyrus the Great

The Last Shah Commemorated Persia's Legacy in 1971

King Cyrus the Great's legacy has worldwide credence and is reinforced by the *Cyropaedia*, written by Xenophon in the 4th century BCE. Xenophon writes an idealized account of the Persian king and extolls his creation of the largest empire in the known world at the time, as well as his central theme of governance that included freedom of religion, freedom of speech, equality of sexes, and respect for other cultures and their traditions.

The somewhat fictionalized *Cyropaedia* is based on firsthand knowledge of the Persian Empire during Xenophon's travels across Persia. He used his personal knowledge and listened to accounts from people who were direct descendants of people who had lived during the reign of Cyrus the Great.

The *Cyropaedia* presents King Cyrus as a virtuous leader, an excellent politician and military strategist, and a man of the people. Based on the writings of Xenophon, Alexander the Great and Julius Caesar both drew on Cyrus's experiences and methods of ruling a vast empire.

The 16th-century depictions of King Cyrus in art show him as one of four great rulers. The other rulers are Ninus of Nineveh (the mythical founder of Nineveh), Alexander, and Julius Caesar.

Thomas Jefferson was a great admirer of Cyrus the Great, and three well-read and marked copies of the *Cyropaedia* were found in his belongings after his death. Benjamin Franklin was another US Founding Father who believed in the principles of Cyrus the Great, as stated in the *Cyropaedia*. Both Jefferson and Franklin saw value and honor in King Cyrus's statecraft, as explained by Xenophon.

King Cyrus is valued as a liberator and benefactor of the Jewish people, especially since he was paramount in the reconstruction of the Temple of Solomon in Jerusalem. The fall of Babylon and setting the Jewish people free made Cyrus a revered figure in Jewish history.

The discovery of the Cyrus Cylinder in 1879 gave the world physical proof that the proclamations of King Cyrus were, in fact, true and not merely biblical or Jewish accounts of stories.

In 1971, the Cyrus Cylinder became an iconic symbol of Iran and was claimed to be the first "charter of human rights" by the last shah of Iran, Mohammad Reza Pahlavi. This modern-day commemoration of the long-ago Persian Empire brought new focus to Cyrus the Great's legacy. It is interesting to note that Reza Shah, the father of Mohammad Reza Pahlavi, requested the name of Persia be changed to Iran in 1941.

The last shah's hopes of resurrecting the Achaemenid era came to an end, as the monarchy was replaced by the Islamic Republic of Iran. Mohammad Reza Pahlavi fled into exile. Many scholars state the shah's rule would not have ended if he had earned the respect of the people and had worked with religious leaders. Iranians wanted greater democracy and less monarchial rule. This might have been possible since the religious leaders wielded great power over the people and could have managed to mediate between the shah and the people.

Shah Mohammad Reza Pahlavi was a Muslim himself but had lost the backing of the clergy of Iran, the Shi'a Muslims, due to his policies of modernization and his relationship with the Israelis. Confrontations with the religious community and an increase in support from the Soviet Union ushered in a time of political unrest.

In August 1953, the streets of Teheran were filled with violence and angry citizens. Fights between rival groups broke out in squares across the city and at the city's major radio station. The home of the prime minister, Mohammad Mossadegh, was protected by armored vehicles and machine guns. Crowds chanted "Zendebad Shah" ("Long live the Shah"), and Mossadegh's government fell. The new government was led by General Fazlollah Zahedi and Shah Mohammed Reza Pahlavi.

Following this coup, the shah spent his time ruling from Iran and maintaining a good relationship with the US until his fall during the Islamic Revolution, which lasted from 1978 to 1979. After ruling for thirty-seven years, the shah and his family fled the country, and the new government converted the country into an Islamic republic.

Islamic Inspiration

In 1978, Shah Mohammed Reza Pahlavi revived the humanitarian legacy of Cyrus the Great by presenting a duplicate of the Cyrus Cylinder to the United Nations to commemorate Cyrus's reign and policies. Unfortunately, the Islamic Revolution was gaining momentum during this time, and in 1979, the Pahlavi rule was overthrown.

After a successful revolution, the Islamic regime wanted the Islamic religion and way of thinking to be accepted by all the Iranian people. In an attempt to mediate, they allowed some pre-Islamic traditions to remain, especially after the death of Ruhollah Khomeini, the first Supreme Leader of the Islamic Republic, in June 1989. Old Persian traditions, such as Noruz or New Year and Chaharshanbeh Suri or the New Year's festival for expelling the Evil Eye from the people, remained.

During the last decade, the Iranian people have started protests at unofficial gatherings to remember Cyrus the Great on October 29th each year. This day was added to the official Iranian calendar in 1977. The protests are aimed against the current government's ideals for religious identity.

On October 29th, 2016, Cyrus the Great Day violence broke out between the Iranian security forces and thousands of civilians who came to celebrate at the tomb of King Cyrus at Pasargadae.

Thousands of citizens rallied together and shouted anti-government slogans. The Iranian regime announced in 2017 that there would be no further festivals at the tomb of Cyrus the Great. Since then, they have had armed forces staffing roadblocks on all major roads leading to the Pasargadae tomb. The situation has been escalating over the years, with over one thousand protesters arrested in the weeks leading up to Cyrus the Great Day in 2022 in various places across the country.

The Fars Province commander of the Revolutionary Guards issued a statement warning that security forces and the judiciary laws would not allow anti-revolutionary forces to gather in the area in celebration of Cyrus the Great Day. He said this would threaten the stability of the region and that measures would be taken to prevent any such gatherings.

Iranian citizens retaliated by starting a social media campaign, inspiring the people of Iran to protest against the autocratic Muslim authorities and continue to celebrate Cyrus the Great Day. This major social media campaign reinforced the historical importance of Cyrus the Great as a national symbol for freedom of religion and freedom of speech. They further denounced the Islamic regime's actions against the celebrations. Social media showed footage of the roadblocks on the main routes. Photographs of civilians crossing the mountains on foot in order to reach the site of the tomb at Pasargadae without using the roads were posted on social media to encourage others to follow.

Further social media comments compared the regime's actions of preventing celebrations on Cyrus the Great Day with the costly efforts used by the regime to encourage pilgrimages to the Muslim holy sites in Iraq. One social media post claimed the regime provided free taxis to the holy sites of Shi'a Muslims during Arba'een, a festival held forty days after Ashura.

The social media campaign provided a platform for people to voice their disagreement with the regime. Opposing forces of the regime used this time to protest the regime. Another post on the social media platform stated, "Today it has been clearly shown that the Islamic Republic and Iran are not the same."

Supporters of the Islamic regime and government policies stated that Cyrus the Great Day was a Western-Zionist plot to undermine the Iranian government and cause harm to Islam.

Ayatollah Ka'abi, a conservative cleric and member of the Assembly of Experts, denounced Cyrus the Great Day in his Friday sermon in Shiraz near the ancient site of Pasargadae and said enemies of Iran and Iranian monarchists created a fake event. The celebration, according to Ayatollah Ka'abi, has no historical proof. In his opinion, the origin was biblical (Jewish) and Israeli and aimed to sow discontent amongst the Iranian people. He continued by saying that Cyrus the Great would convert to Islam if he rose from his grave and saw the power of Iran under Islamic rule.

Mehran Solati, a prominent sociologist, stated that the prevention of celebrations on Cyrus the Great Day is comparable to the shah's efforts to erase Islam, which failed. Solati further said the constant social media discussions reinforced the pre-Islamic culture and identity, even though the regime is trying to Islamize the population.

According to Tabnak, a Persian news website, there is an increased interest in the celebrations of Cyrus the Great Day amongst the people of Iran. People believe the steps taken by the regime are ineffective. An alternative view on this is that the regime should view the respect the people have for the founder of the Persian Empire, Cyrus the Great, as an opportunity to strengthen national solidarity and sentiment instead of seeing it as a threat to national security.

Iranian police barred people from visiting the mausoleum in October 2021, and although Cyrus the Great Day remains an unofficial celebration on the calendar, we are not sure what will happen to it in the future.

Conclusion

The Fascinating Conundrums of Reconstructing Ancient Histories

The accounts of ancient civilizations passed down to us by ancient historians vary greatly. It is understandably influenced by the time and space between the actual occurrences and their recording.

The so-called father of history, Herodotus, relied on accounts of descendants, but even then, he admits that he is recording what he heard and not what he had seen. He often interweaves the mythology and belief systems of the subject matter with his own Greek cultural interpretations. He was fascinated with the Persians, especially the wars of the Persians against the Greeks, and obtained much of his information from second-generation accounts. Thus, he was much closer in time to the actual wars than the later accounts of Xenophon and others.

On the other hand, Xenophon was directly involved with the Persians, as he became the commander of the most elite Persian military unit, The Immortals, which, if you don't recall, were ten thousand crack troops. At this time (c. 401 BCE), the unit was largely made up of Greek mercenaries. Xenophon was gifted and accomplished as a military leader, philosopher, and historian. His account of Cyrus in the *Cyropaedia* is, however, an attempt at biographical fiction akin to hero worship, which is not surprising if we remember that the King of Kings, Cyrus himself, was born nearly two centuries before Xenophon.

Another ancient writer of the history of the Persians was Ctesias. He was a physician at the Achaemenid court around 400 BCE, acting as the personal doctor of the king and his family. He wrote twenty-three books called the *Persica* on the history of Persia up to that time. Despite it being relatively close to the era of Cyrus and his direct descendants, his accounts differ greatly from those of Herodotus and Xenophon. This may be due to the fact that the line of kings that he served was from a different branch of the Achaemenid dynasty, which started with Darius I.

Ctesias's original work did not survive, but several ancient writers refer to and quote directly from it. Of the twenty-three books, five were apparently devoted to Cyrus the Great. But even the ancient authors criticize Ctesias heavily, as he was more interested in court intrigues, harem scandals, and romances at court than in facts of historical importance.

One significant aspect where Ctesias differs greatly from Herodotus is the lineage of Cyrus. Ctesias states Cyrus was the son of a female shepherd or goatherd named Argoste and a male bandit named Artadates. Cyrus became Astyages's cupbearer, then conspired with the Persians, overthrew Astyages, and became king in his stead. What is fascinating about Ctesias's version of Cyrus's story is the obvious similarities to the birth, youth, and rise to kingship of Sargon the Great, the founder of the Akkadian Empire, which fell more than a thousand years before Cyrus's birth. However, the future empire builder Sargon was raised by the king's gardener instead of a goatherd! Incidentally, this kind of legend was spun more than once in the case of hero figures in ancient times.

It, therefore, remains an intricate endeavor for any modern scholar to extract and balance fact from fiction when it comes to these ancient written documents, the records of other contemporary nations, and archaeological, linguistic, and even genetic data. In the case of the Medes, for example, the meager knowledge of their existence has been enhanced by more archaeological excavations and discoveries during the past few years. We have to bear in mind that the climatic conditions of most of the geographical areas in which Cyrus and the Achaemenids held sway often prevented the preservation of written documents—both the ink and the vellum or other materials on which it was written—unlike those inscribed with a stylus on wet clay or inscriptions on monuments or stelae.

Admired by Enemies

The Nabonidus Chronicle is the primary source of information for this period and gives a good account of Cyrus's rise to power and his conquest of the Medes. It describes his destruction and plunder of Ecbatana, which had been the capital and home of Astyages. Here, we get a glimpse into Cyrus's mind as he dethrones Astyages; according to Herodotus, Astyages lives at the court of Cyrus until his death. Ctesias, however, states that Astyages was given a province to rule in the region of Parthia but died when a neighboring province invaded.

Capturing King Croesus of Lydia was the foremost in Cyrus's mind when it came to conquest. After capturing Croesus, the former Lydian king asked Cyrus to allow him to live. Cyrus, always the forward thinker, considered what would happen to him if he was in the same position as Croesus. This made him reconsider lighting the pyre Croesus was on, and subsequently, Croesus became one of his major advisors in military conquests.

Wise and Charismatic but Not Infallible

Throughout his reign, Cyrus the Great displayed charisma and skill on all levels, social and political. A great example is when he wanted to expand his empire into the steppes. He considered a more diplomatic approach and asked Queen Tomyris to marry him.

Tomyris was also a skilled and clever ruler in her own right. She was also a skilled warrior on horseback. She knew the proposal from Cyrus only meant he wanted her land. In the end, King Cyrus, who was initially quite content with what he had already achieved, was enticed into battle by his ambition for more land, despite his abhorrence and lifelong abstinence from greed. It cost him his life.

It Is a Wrap

Of all the rulers in the ancient and current world, King Cyrus deserves the title "Great" attached to his name due to his success and skill. He pursued a policy of ruling by generosity and tolerance. During King Cyrus's rule, there were no rebellions of satrapies or regions since Cyrus managed his empire like a good CEO would manage a large company in modern times. He had advisory boards, imperial courts, and governments and allowed them to function as part of the empire with responsibilities for their own regions. This gave them the autonomy they needed to feel in control. Cyrus knew on an instinctual level that rulers needed to feel empowered and act as guardians of their own territories. By fulfilling this basic need, he could be assured of their loyalty. His assumptions proved true.

Professor Richard Frye, Professor Emeritus of Iranian Studies at Harvard University, had this to say about Cyrus the Great and his legacy:

"In short, the figure of Cyrus has survived throughout history as more than a great man who founded an empire. He became the epitome of the great qualities expected of a ruler in antiquity, and he assumed heroic features as a conqueror who was tolerant and magnanimous as well as brave and daring. His personality as seen by the Greeks, influenced them and Alexander the Great, and, as the tradition was transmitted by the Romans, may be considered to influence our thinking even now." ("Cyrus the Great and Religious Tolerance in Achaemenid Persia")

Continuing to extol his virtues would be unnecessary. We have seen through our journey back in time that this man was unique. He was indeed worthy of his title Cyrus the Great!

Here's another book by Enthralling History that you might like

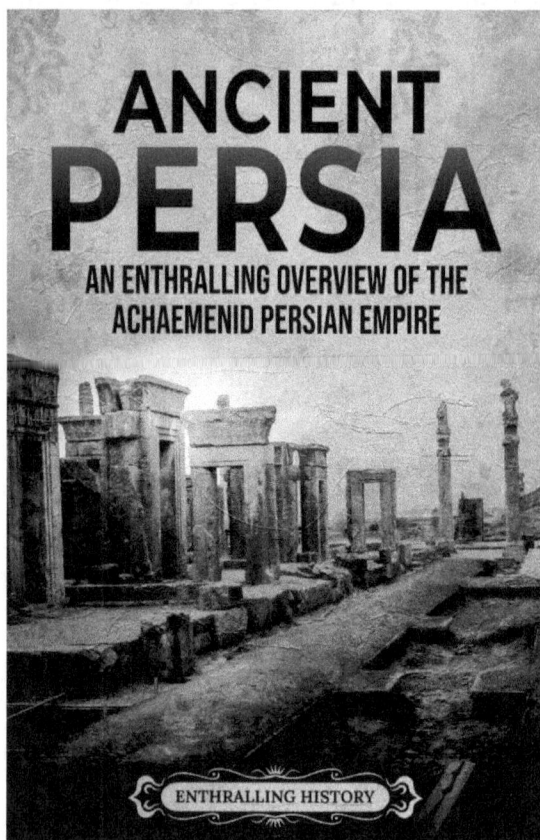

ANCIENT
PERSIA
AN ENTHRALLING OVERVIEW OF THE
ACHAEMENID PERSIAN EMPIRE

ENTHRALLING HISTORY

Free limited time bonus

Stop for a moment. We have a free bonus set up for you. The problem is this: we forget 90% of everything that we read after 7 days. Crazy fact, right? Here's the solution: we've created a printable, 1-page pdf summary for this book that you're reading now. All you have to do to get your free pdf summary is to go to the following website: **https://livetolearn.lpages.co/enthrallinghistory/**

Once you do, it will be intuitive. Enjoy, and thank you!

We forget 90% of everything
that we've read in 7 days...

Get the free printable pdf summary of
the book you've read AND much, much
more... shhhh...

Enter Your Most Frequently Used Email to Get Started

**DOWNLOAD FREE PDF
SUMMARY**

© Enthralling History

Cyrus the Great – Reference List

The Project Gutenberg eBook of Cyrus the Great, Makers Of History, by Jacob Abbott.

"Who was Cyrus the Great? - Culture." 06 May. 2019, https://www.nationalgeographic.com/culture/article/cyrus-the-great.

"Cyrus the Great | Biography & Facts | Britannica." 20 Oct. 2022, https://www.britannica.com/biography/Cyrus-the-Great.

"Cyrus the Great — M. Rahim Shayegan | Harvard University Press." 02 Apr. 2019, https://www.hup.harvard.edu/catalog.php?isbn=9780674987388.

"Cyrus The Great." https://cyrusthegreat.net/index.html.

"HOME | Cyrus the Great." https://www.cyrusthegreatstory.com/.

"History of Iran: Cyropaedia of Xenophon; The Life of Cyrus the Great." 19 Oct. 2022, https://www.iranchamber.com/history/xenophon/cyropaedia_xenophon_book1.php.

"Xenophon's Cyrus the Great: the arts of leadership and war." 25 Jan. 2022, https://archive.org/details/xenophonscyrusgr0000xeno.

"Leadership and 'The Art of War' - Ivey Business School." 03 Mar. 2022, https://www.ivey.uwo.ca/leadership/for-leaders/leadership-blogs/2022/03/leadership-and-the-art-of-war/.

"CYRUS ACCORDING TO HERODOTUS – Encyclopedia Iranica." 15 Dec. 2003, https://www.iranicaonline.org/articles/herodotus-iv.

"Herodotus on Cyrus' capture of Babylon - Livius."
https://www.livius.org/sources/content/herodotus/cyrus-takes-babylon/.

"Herodotus and Xenophon. - Bible Hub."
https://biblehub.com/library/abbott/cyrus_the_great/chapter_i_herodotus_
and_xenophon.htm.

"Histories | Book 1, The Rise of Cyrus the Great | Summary."
https://www.coursehero.com/lit/Histories/book-1-the-rise-of-cyrus-the-
great-summary/.

"HERODOTUS BOOK 1: CYRUS THE GREAT AND RISE OF
PERSIA."
http://www.christophergennari.com/uploads/2/3/9/9/2399857/herodotus_
on_early_cyrus.pdf.

"Herodotus, bk 1, logos 2 - Livius."
https://www.livius.org/sources/about/herodotus/herodotus bk 1-logos-2/.

"Herodotus (5) - Livius." 16 Apr. 2020,
https://www.livius.org/articles/person/herodotus/herodotus-5/.

"THE EKTHESIS OF CYRUS THE GREAT: A CASE STUDY OF
HEROICITY VERSUS." 27 Feb. 2017,
https://www.cambridge.org/core/journals/cambridge-classical-
journal/article/ekthesis-of-cyrus-the-great-a-case-study-of-heroicity-versus-
bastardy-in-classical-athens/9809094BB9FAC1DC67F7CB32C3D02890.

"Cyrus the Great - Livius." 12 Oct. 2020,
https://www.livius.org/articles/person/cyrus-the-great/.

"Herodotus: The defeat of the Persians under Cyrus the Great by Queen."
https://www.cais-
soas.com/CAIS/History/hakhamaneshian/herod_tomyr.htm.

"Cyrus the Great's Accomplishments & Major Achievements - Totally
History." https://totallyhistory.com/cyrus-the-greats-accomplishments/.

"CYROPAEDIA – Encyclopedia Iranica."
https://iranicaonline.org/articles/cyropaedia-gr.

Cyrus the Great and Religious Tolerance,
https://tolerance.tavaana.org/en/content/cyrus-great-and-religious-
tolerance.

"Cyropaedia | work by Xenophon | Britannica."
https://www.britannica.com/topic/Cyropaedia.

"Cyropaedia, by Xenophon - Project Gutenberg." 18 Jul. 2009,
https://gutenberg.org/files/2085/2085-h/2085-h.htm.

"Cyropaedia: Xenophon: Free Download, Borrow, and Streaming:
Internet." https://archive.org/details/cyropaediavolum00millgoog.

"Cyropaedia (The Education of Cyrus) Background | GradeSaver."
https://www.gradesaver.com/cyropaedia-the-education-of-cyrus.

"Cyrus' Paradise | The World's First Online Collaborative Commentary."
http://cyropaedia.online/.

"Cyropaedia Summary - eNotes.com." 06 May. 2015,
https://www.enotes.com/topics/cyropaedia.

"Achaemenid Empire - Wikipedia."
https://en.wikipedia.org/wiki/Achaemenid_Empire.

"Achaemenid Empire Timeline - World History Encyclopedia."
https://www.worldhistory.org/timeline/Achaemenid_Empire/.

"The Achaemenid Empire | World Civilization - Lumen Learning."
https://courses.lumenlearning.com/suny-hccc-
worldcivilization/chapter/the-achaemenid-empire/.

"History of Iran: Achaemenid Empire - Iran Chamber."
https://www.iranchamber.com/history/achaemenids/achaemenids.php."Th
e Achaemenid Persian Empire (550–330 B.C.) - The Met's Heilbrunn."
https://www.metmuseum.org/toah/hd/acha/hd_acha.htm.

"Achaemenid Empire - World History Maps."
https://www.worldhistorymaps.info/civilizations/achaemenid-empire/.

"Persian Empire | History of the Achaemenid Persian Empire."
https://persianempire.org/.

"Achaemenid Empire | Ancient Persia Wiki | Fandom."
https://ancientpersia.fandom.com/wiki/Achaemenid_Empire.

"Persian Empire | National Geographic Society." 20 May. 2022,
https://education.nationalgeographic.org/resource/persian-empire/.

"The Culture, People & Daily Life of Ancient Persia - Study.com." 13
Mar. 2022, https://study.com/learn/lesson/ancient-persia-clothing-people-
daily-life.html.

"Ancient Persian Culture - World History Encyclopedia." 27 Nov. 2019,
https://www.worldhistory.org/Ancient_Persian_Culture/.

"Ancient Persia - World History Encyclopedia." 12 Nov. 2019,
https://www.worldhistory.org/Persia/.

"Persian Empire - HISTORY." 25 Jan. 2018,
https://www.history.com/topics/ancient-middle-east/persian-empire.

"Ancient Persia: 12 Major Events - World History Edu." 02 Nov. 2021,
https://www.worldhistoryedu.com/ancient-persia-12-major-events/.

"Who were the ancient Persians? | Live Science." 02 Mar. 2022,
https://www.livescience.com/who-were-the-persians.

"Ancient Persia: The Achaemenid Empire to the History of Iran." 02 Feb. 2019, https://historycooperative.org/history-of-iran/.

"42 Astounding Facts About Life in Ancient Persia - Factinate." https://www.factinate.com/things/42-astounding-facts-life-ancient-persia/.

"Persians - Wikipedia." https://en.wikipedia.org/wiki/Persians.

"Persia: Ancient Iran and the Classical World - Getty Museum." https://www.getty.edu/art/exhibitions/persia/explore.html.

"Persian Empire | National Geographic Society." 20 May. 2022, https://www.nationalgeographic.org/encyclopedia/persian-empire/.

"Ancient Iran | History, Map, Cities, Religion, Art, Language, & Facts." https://www.britannica.com/place/ancient-Iran.

"Ancient Persia - ancient.com." https://ancient.com/category/articles/ancient-countries/ancient-persia/.

"Satrap - Wikipedia." https://en.wikipedia.org/wiki/Satrap.

"Satrap Definition & Meaning - Merriam-Webster." https://www.merriam-webster.com/dictionary/satrap.

"satrap | Persian provincial governor | Britannica." https://www.britannica.com/topic/satrap.

"Satrap - Encyclopedia of The Bible - Bible Gateway." https://www.biblegateway.com/resources/encyclopedia-of-the-bible/Satrap.

"Satrap | Encyclopedia.com." https://www.encyclopedia.com/history/asia-and-africa/ancient-history-middle-east/satrap.

"Who were the satraps in the book of Daniel? | GotQuestions.org." 04 Jan. 2022, https://www.gotquestions.org/satraps-Daniel.html.

"Satrap — Watchtower ONLINE LIBRARY - JW.ORG." https://wol.jw.org/en/wol/d/r1/lp-e/1200003846.

"Twelve Great Women of Ancient Persia - World History Encyclopedia." 31 Jan. 2020, https://www.worldhistory.org/article/1493/twelve-great-women-of-ancient-persia/.

"Women in Ancient Persia - World History Encyclopedia." 30 Jan. 2020, https://www.worldhistory.org/article/1492/women-in-ancient-persia/.

"Women in Ancient Persia - World History Encyclopedia." 30 Jan. 2020, https://www.worldhistory.org/article/1492/women-in-ancient-persia/.

"Women Warriors: The Ancient Female Fighters That Ruled Persia." 04 Aug. 2020, https://historythings.com/women-warriors-ancient-female-fighters-ruled-persia/.

"What Life Was Like for Women in Ancient Persia - Grunge.com." 19 Jul. 2020, https://www.grunge.com/227986/what-life-was-like-for-women-in-ancient-persia/.

"Women in Ancient Persia - Brewminate: A Bold Blend of News and Ideas." 02 Feb. 2020, https://brewminate.com/women-in-ancient-persia/.

"PERSIA WOMEN WARRIORS - ROOTSHUNT." https://rootshunt.com/aryans/bharatpersiawomenwarriors/persiawomenwarriors/persiawomenwarriors.htm.

"Warrior Women of the Ancient World - ThoughtCo." 11 Jul. 2019, https://www.thoughtco.com/ancient-women-warriors-121482.

"MASSAGETAE – Encyclopedia Iranica." https://www.iranicaonline.org/articles/massagetae.

"Massagetae Tribe And Its Queen Tomyris." 18 Nov. 2019, https://www.ancientpages.com/2019/11/18/massagetae-warlike-and-brave-nomadic-tribe-of-central-asia/.

"The Massagetae (Tomyris) - Civilization V Customisation Wiki." 27 Feb. 2015, https://civilization-v-customisation.fandom.com/wiki/The_Massagetae_(Tomyris).

"Tomyris: The cut-throat warrior queen of Massagetae." 20 Oct. 2022, https://www.history101.com/tomyris-queen-of-massagetae/.

"Massagetae — Google Arts & Culture." https://artsandculture.google.com/entity/massagetae/m04p9wr?hl=en.

"Achaemenid Persian Empire | Massagetae - Arcadian Venture LLC." https://persianempire.org/cultures/massagetae.

"Massagetes - Livius." https://www.livius.org/articles/people/massagetes/.

The Legend of Tomiris (2019). Movie.

"Tomyris, The Female Warrior and Ruler Who May Have Killed Cyrus the Great." 26 Feb. 2016, https://www.ancient-origins.net/history-famous-people/tomyris-female-warrior-and-ruler-who-may-have-killed-cyrus-great-005423.

"Tomyris - Wikipedia." https://en.wikipedia.org/wiki/Tomyris.

"Civilization VI: Leader Spotlight - Tomyris - YouTube." https://www.youtube.com/watch?v=zCGNMBi0O3c.

"Cyrus the Great and Persian control of the Middle East." 16 Jan. 2020, https://www.deseret.com/2020/1/16/21065608/daniel-peterson-cyrus-the-great-and-persian-control-of-the-middle-east.

"Cyrus the Great Day: Between Iranian and Islamic Identities." 28 Nov. 2017, https://dayan.org/content/cyrus-great-day-between-iranian-and-islamic-identities.

"Cyrus the Great Captures Babylon | History on This Day." 16 Dec. 2019, https://historyonthisday.com/events/middle-east/cyrus-the-great-captures-babylon/.

"Iranians arrested after celebrating ancient Persian king Cyrus the Great." 31 Oct. 2016, https://www.jpost.com/Middle-East/Iranians-arrested-after-celebrating-ancient-Persian-king-Cyrus-the-Great-471309.

"Pasargadae - Wikipedia." https://en.wikipedia.org/wiki/Pasargadae"

Darius the Great - Wikipedia." https://en.wikipedia.org/wiki/Darius_the_Great.

"Darius the Great - Wikipedia." https://en.wikipedia.org/wiki/Darius_the_Great.

"Darius I of Persia – Amazing Bible Timeline with World History." 25 Nov. 2012, https://amazingbibletimeline.com/blog/darius-i-of-persia/. org/wiki/Pasargadae.

"Pasargadae - UNESCO World Heritage Centre." https://whc.unesco.org/en/list/1106.

"PASARGADAE – Encyclopedia Iranica." https://www.iranicaonline.org/articles/pasargadae.

"Pasargadae | ancient city, Iran | Britannica." https://www.britannica.com/place/Pasargadae-ancient-city-Iran.

"Pasargadae - History and Facts | History Hit." 18 Jun. 2021, https://www.historyhit.com/locations/pasargadae/.

"Home [https://www.pasargadae.info/fa/]." https://www.pasargadae.info/en/.

"Pasargadae - Amazing Facts, History, Site Map - Iran Safar." 13 Nov. 2021, https://www.iransafar.co/pasargadae-ultimate-guide/.

"Pasargadae - BiblePlaces.com." https://www.bibleplaces.com/pasargadae/.

"Darius (c.-550 - -486) - Genealogy - geni family tree." 18 Jun. 2004, https://www.geni.com/people/Darius-I-the-Great-King-of-Persia/6000000006131567298.

"Pasargadae - World Archaeology." 20 Sept. 2019, https://www.world-archaeology.com/features/pasargadae/.

"Pasargadae | Visit Iran." https://www.visitiran.ir/attraction/pasargadae.

"Pasargadae - UNESCO World Heritage Site | Iran Destination | Iran Tour." https://www.irandestination.com/pasargadae/.

"Pasargadae, Fars Province | Ultimate Guide | Photos - Iran Tourismer." 01 May. 2019, https://irantourismer.com/pasargadae-tomb-of-cyrus/.

"Pasargadae | The Tomb of Cyrus, the Great | Shiraz Attraction - Apochi." https://apochi.com/attractions/shiraz/pasargadae/.

"Pasargadae – Welcome to Iran." https://welcometoiran.com/pasargadae/.

"Cyrus Cylinder - Livius." 12 Oct. 2020, https://www.livius.org/sources/content/cyrus-cylinder/.

"Cyrus Cylinder - Wikipedia." https://en.wikipedia.org/wiki/Cyrus_Cylinder.

"The Cyrus Cylinder - World History Encyclopedia." 18 Jan. 2012, https://www.worldhistory.org/article/166/the-cyrus-cylinder/.

"10 Facts About the Cyrus Cylinder | Asia Society." https://asiasociety.org/northern-california/10-facts-about-cyrus-cylinder.

"What is the Cyrus Cylinder and why does it matter? – BibleMesh." 26 Jul. 2019, https://biblemesh.com/blog/what-is-the-cyrus-cylinder-and-why-does-it-matter/.

"What is the Cyrus Cylinder? - CYRUS CYLINDER FOR PEACE & HUMAN RIGHTS." 20 Apr. 2021, https://cyruscylinderforpeace.org/what-is-the-cyrus-cylinder/.

"CYRUS CYLINDER FOR PEACE & HUMAN RIGHTS." https://cyruscylinderforpeace.org/.

"Cyrus Cylinder - Bible History." https://bible-history.com/archaeology/cyrus-cylinder.

"cylinder | British Museum." https://www.britishmuseum.org/collection/object/W_1880-0617-1941.

"The Cyrus Cylinder - Tyndale House." https://academic.tyndalehouse.com/explore/articles/the-cyrus-cylinder/.

"The Cyrus Cylinder - Tyndale House." https://tyndalehouse.com/explore/articles/the-cyrus-cylinder/.

"History of Iran: Cyrus the Great - Iran Chamber." https://www.iranchamber.com/history/cyrus/cyrus.php.

"History of Iran: The Cyrus the Great Cylinder - Iran Chamber." 22 Oct. 2022, https://www.iranchamber.com/history/cyrus/cyrus_charter.php.

"History of Iran: Cyropaedia of Xenophon, The Life of Cyrus the Great." https://mail.iranchamber.com/history/xenophon/cyropaedia_xenophon_book2.php.

"Cyrus the Great - The History Files." https://www.historyfiles.co.uk/FeaturesMiddEast/EasternPersiaKings.htm.

"The Importance of Cyrus the Great in Iranian History - Destination Iran." 04 Mar. 2015, https://www.destinationiran.com/importance-of-cyrus-the-great-in-iranian-history.htm.

"History of Iran: Cyrus the Great: The decree of return for the Jews." https://www.iranchamber.com/history/cyrus/cyrus_decree_jews.php.

"Iran Regime's Panic and Fear From the Ceremony of Cyrus the Great." 28 Oct. 2017, https://www.ncr-iran.org/en/news/society/iran-regime-s-panic-and-fear-from-the-ceremony-of-cyrus-the-great/.

"The Persian Empire: Culture and Society | TimeMaps." https://www.timemaps.com/encyclopedia/persian-empire-culture-society/.

"Persepolis - Wikipedia." https://en.wikipedia.org/wiki/Persepolis.

"Persepolis - UNESCO World Heritage Centre." https://whc.unesco.org/en/list/114.

"PERSEPOLIS – Encyclopedia Iranica." https://www.iranicaonline.org/articles/persepolis.

"The Conquest of Babylon. - Bible Hub." https://biblehub.com/library/abbott/cyrus_the_great/chapter_viii_the_conquest_of.htm.

"Fall of Babylon - Wikipedia." https://en.wikipedia.org/wiki/Fall_of_Babylon.

"How Cyrus Conquered Babylon: God's Kingdom Ministries." 01 Jun. 2015, https://godskingdom.org/studies/ffi-newsletter/2015/how-cyrus-conquered-babylon.

"Babylonian captivity - Wikipedia." https://en.wikipedia.org/wiki/Babylonian_captivity.

"History of Babylon in the Bible - Learn Religions." 04 Dec. 2019, https://www.learnreligions.com/history-of-babylon-3867031.

"The Bible Journey | Assyria is conquered by the Babylonians." 26 Jul. 2015, https://www.thebiblejourney.org/biblejourney2/33-judah-after-the-fall-of-israel/assyria-is-conquered-by-the-babylonians/.

"Babylonia and the Conquest of Judah." 13 Apr. 2021, https://www.churchofjesuschrist.org/study/manual/old-testament-student-manual-kings-malachi/enrichment-g?lang=eng.

"Nabonidus - Wikipedia." https://en.wikipedia.org/wiki/Nabonidus.

"Archaeologists Find Inscribed Stone Honoring Babylonian King Nabonidus." 22 Jul. 2021, https://www.ancient-origins.net/news-history-archaeology/nabonidus-0015607.

"The Last King of Babylon - Archaeology Magazine."
https://www.archaeology.org/issues/458-2203/features/10334-babylon-nabonidus-last-king.

"NABONIDUS, BELSHAZZAR, AND THE BOOK OF DANIEL: AN UPDATE." https://www.biblia.work/sermons/nabonidusbelshazzar-and-the-book-of-daniel-an-update/.

"The Babylonian King Nabonidus - World History Encyclopedia." 22 Mar. 2018, https://www.worldhistory.org/image/8412/the-babylonian-king-nabonidus/.

"Nabonidus Cylinder, Text | Mesopotamian Gods & Kings." 01 May. 2018, http://www.mesopotamiangods.com/nabonidus-cylinder-text/.

"Cambyses II | king of Persia | Britannica." https://www.britannica.com/biography/Cambyses-II.

"Cambyses II - Wikipedia." https://en.wikipedia.org/wiki/Cambyses_II.

"Cambyses - Encyclopedia of The Bible - Bible Gateway." https://www.biblegateway.com/resources/encyclopedia-of-the-bible/Cambyses.

"The Story of the Lost Army of Cambyses - Jay Penner." 21 Oct. 2019, https://www.jaypenner.com/blog/the-story-of-the-lost-army-of-cambyses.

"Lost Army of Cambyses - Wikipedia." https://en.wikipedia.org/wiki/Lost_Army_of_Cambyses.

"Mysterious Death Of Cambyses II - Ancient Pages." 21 Apr. 2021, https://www.ancientpages.com/2021/04/21/mysterious-death-of-cambyses-ii-natural-suicide-or-assassination-by-darius-i-the-great/.

"Cambyses II - Livius." https://www.livius.org/articles/person/cambyses-ii/.

"CAMBYSES – Encyclopedia Iranica." 15 Dec. 1990, https://www.iranicaonline.org/articles/cambyses-opers.

"Persian Emperors List & Timeline | Cyrus, Cambyses II & Darius - Study.com." 11 Apr. 2022, https://study.com/academy/lesson/kings-of-the-persian-empire-cyrus-cambyses-ii-darius-i.html.

"Ezra on Cyrus - Livius." https://www.livius.org/sources/content/bible/ezra-on-cyrus/.

"Ezra 1 NIV - Cyrus Helps the Exiles to Return - Bible Gateway." https://www.biblegateway.com/passage/?search=Ezra%201&version=NIV.

"Ezra 1:1-11 – Cyrus's Decree - Enter the Bible." https://enterthebible.org/passage/ezra-11-11-cyruss-decree.

"Ezra in the Bible - Who Was He and What Did He Do - Crosswalk.com." 21 Sept. 2021, https://www.crosswalk.com/faith/bible-study/important-things-we-can-learn-from-the-book-of-ezra.html.

"Ezra 1 - In the first year of Cyrus king of Persia..."
https://www.esv.org/Ezra+1/.

"Enduring Word Bible Commentary Ezra Chapter 1."
https://enduringword.com/bible-commentary/ezra-1/.

"Daniel and King Cyrus - Biblical Hermeneutics Stack Exchange." 30 Sept.
2021, https://hermeneutics.stackexchange.com/questions/69453/daniel-
and-king-cyrus.

"Who was Cyrus in the Bible? | GotQuestions.org." 04 Jan. 2022,
https://www.gotquestions.org/Cyrus-Bible.html.

"Daniel (biblical figure) - Wikipedia."
https://en.wikipedia.org/wiki/Daniel_(biblical_figure).

"Daniel 10:1 In the third year of Cyrus king of Persia..."
https://biblehub.com/daniel/10-1.htm.

"Daniel and Darius - Israel My Glory."
https://israelmyglory.org/article/daniel-and-darius/.

"Daniel and Cyrus Before the Idol Bel - Google Arts & Culture."
https://artsandculture.google.com/asset/daniel-and-cyrus-before-the-idol-
bel-rembrandt-harmensz-van-rijn/bQEZf5tgp8ZerQ?hl=en.

www.ingramcontent.com/pod-product-compliance
Lightning Source LLC
LaVergne TN
LVHW051745080426
835511LV00018B/3231